Great

Crazy British Movies

Great British Movies

Don Shiach

www.pocketessentials.com

First published in 2006 by Pocket Essentials
P.O.Box 394, Harpenden, Herts, AL5 1XJ
www.pocketessentials.com

A CIP catalogue record for this book is available from the British Library.

ISBN-10: 1 904048 59 5
EAN-13: 978 1 904048 59 6

2 4 6 8 10 9 7 5 3 1

Typeset by Avocet Typeset, Chilton, Aylesbury, Bucks
Printed and bound in Great Britain by Cox & Wyman, Reading

Contents

Introduction

François Truffaut, the French director and critic, famously once said that the cinema and the British were inimical to one another, implying that as a nation we had neither a real cinematic tradition nor an innate feel for cinema, a summation that was clearly partial and superficial. In tandem with other French directors and critics of the 'nouvelle vague' era, Truffaut was a Hollywood enthusiast, often elevating routine material to the level of art and discovering hitherto hidden directorial 'geniuses' such as Howard Hawks, Samuel Fuller and even Jerry Lewis as justification of the 'auteur theory', which established the director as the author of a film. However, it is true that throughout its history British cinema has had to contend with the increasingly dominating influence of the Hollywood industry. At times it has struggled to survive, not only in an artistic sense but also as a separate economic entity, raising the question of whether or not there has existed an indigenous film industry at all.

With this Hollywood dominance of the marketplace has come an economic stranglehold, easily imposed by the major American film companies. More and more, the problem has been how a truly British film industry could make British films that reflected British society, and avoid merely producing genre product for a worldwide market in which 95% of the films shown were made by American companies or financed by American money. What is, after all, a 'British film'? For example, three of the most successful 'British' films of all time — *The Bridge on the River Kwai*, *Lawrence of Arabia* and *The English Patient* — were all financed by Hollywood money, but they are largely British in content and have British directors, writers and stars. For the purposes of this book, the selection of films I have made to represent the best of British cinema is defined by how British the subject-matter is and the national identity of the major artistic influences.

Seventy-odd movies have been chosen for individual treatment, and obviously any such selection depends on personal taste and predilection. James Bond fans may be outraged that no single Bond film makes the list, as will 'Carry On' devotees. Whilst there is no doubt that both these series are significant in the history of the British film industry, my ultimate criteria have been significance and artistic merit. When the total oeuvre of the British film industry is considered, it is possible to see how Truffaut's statement about the British and cinema can be dismissed as critically insubstantial.

Finding its Feet: 1926–39

The silent era in cinema produced few memorable British movies, one exception being *The Lodger*, directed by a young Alfred Hitchcock, who made his mark with this film as a director of imagination and individuality. However, with the success of *The Jazz Singer*, and Hollywood's subsequent wholesale investment in sound stages and movies, the indigenous industry faced the same problems then that it would for the rest of the twentieth century and into the new millennium: how to compete with the Hollywood monster.

Two individuals dominate this period of British film history, Hitchcock and Alexander Korda, a native Hungarian, who nevertheless became wholly identified with the attempt to create a homegrown industry that could rival Hollywood and at the same time make worthwhile films of some artistic merit. In addition to this strand of commercial filmmaking, there emerged a strong documentary tradition under the aegis of John Grierson at the GPO Film Unit and Edgar Anstey at British Transport. As well as making memorable single documentary films such as *Drifters* and *Night Mail*, these pioneers had a lasting influence on British 'realist' movies in later decades.

British stars such as Ronald Colman, Charles Laughton, Laurence Olivier and Vivien Leigh were snapped up by Hollywood and became international box-office attractions. However, in Britain there was still the prevalent view that the cinema was an inferior art to the theatre and many British 'names' perceived work in the films as 'slumming it'. Too many British films of this era looked to the theatre for its material, stars and inspiration, so the history of the British cinema in the 1930s is littered with forgettable farces, dire musicals, drawing-room comedies à la Noel Coward and damp squib thrillers. Top box-office stars of this period included Jessie Matthews, George Formby and Will Hay. Nevertheless, the movies discussed in this section pay tribute to the fact that some innovators were thinking outside those particular boxes and in so doing, made movies of some lasting merit.

Blackmail (1929)

Crew: directed by Alfred Hitchcock; produced by John Maxwell; screenplay by Alfred Hitchcock, Benn W Levy and Charles Bennett, based on the play by Charles Bennett; cinematography by Jack Cox; music by John Hubert Bath, Henry Stafford and John Reynders; edited by Emil De Ruelle. B&W. 75 mins.

Cast: Anny Ondra (Alice White); John Longden (Frank Webber); Donald Calthrop (Tracy); Cyril Ritchard (The Artist); Sara Allgood (Mrs White); Charles Paton (Mr White).

Blackmail is not only interesting as one of Hitchcock's earliest successes, it stands as an important milestone in the history of British cinema. It was originally shot as a silent movie, but the arrival of sound technology and the subsequent banishment to history of silent cinema demanded that the film be transformed into a 'talkie'. Hitchcock shot new scenes with sound and dubbed the existing footage. Thus, the film was seen in Britain as a silent movie in many cinemas and as the first all-talkie British movie in some newly equipped theatres.

The story is about a young woman whose boyfriend is a Scotland Yard detective. She becomes involved with an artist who has designs on her and tries to force her to pose nude for him, whereupon she stabs him to death. To add to her problems, her boyfriend leads the investigation into the crime and she becomes the object of blackmail. Hitchcock initially wanted the film to end with the young woman locked up in jail, but was persuaded to substitute a conventionally happy conclusion.

This rather trite melodramatic plot allows Hitchcock to explore recurring themes: woman as the object of voyeuristic lust, sexual guilt and the transference of guilt, and redemption. Clearly influenced in his early days by German expressionism and directors such as Fritz Lang, FW Murnau and GW Pabst, *Blackmail* is a cut above other British films of this period: layers of meaning are brought to relatively conventional material and pure cinematic devices enhance and give depth to the narrative. The added dialogue is not of great importance; it is the use of composition within the frame, point-of-view camera techniques and camera angles in general, the lighting, close-ups and the sound effects used, that mark this movie as the work of a cinematic genius in the making. Eighty years on, the movie inevitably seems creaky at times, especially considering that the soundtrack was added after the silent version was shot and the lead actress's lines had to be dubbed (Anny Ondra was Polish and English actress Joan Barry read her lines for her).

The *Lodger* (1926), starring Ivor Novello, had already announced Alfred Hitchcock as a major talent of the burgeoning British film industry. *Blackmail* reinforced his reputation as an innovative director who was willing to handle darker themes than mass audience cinema usually allowed. He adapted expressionistic techniques from art movies to this commercial product, that presaged how later in his Hollywood career he would bestride the worlds of the commercial and the art house movie, resulting in his reputation, not only among general cinemagoers, but also those interested in 'serious' cinema. *Blackmail* remains a landmark in British cinema history and is still well worth viewing to the present day.

The Private Life of Henry VIII (1933)

Crew: directed by Alexander Korda; produced by Alexander Korda and Ludovico Toeplitz; screenplay by Lajos Biro and Arthur Wimperis; cinematography by Georges Perinal; music by Kurt Schroeder; edited by Harold Young and Stephen Harrison; art direction by Vincent Korda. B&W. 97 mins.

Cast: Charles Laughton (Henry VIII); Robert Donat (Robert Culpepper); Binnie Barnes (Katherine Howard); Elsa Lanchester (Anne of Cleves); Merle Oberon (Anne Boleyn); Wendy Barrie (Jane Seymour); Everley Gregg (Catherine Parr); Franklin Dyall (Thomas Cromwell).

Alexander Korda was a Hungarian who had worked prolifically in the Hungarian, French and German cinemas before settling in Britain and attempting to make movies in English that would break into the lucrative American market and help to establish the British film industry as a rival to Hollywood. He formed a production company called London Films, which made *The Private Life of Henry VIII* and would play a central role in creating an important native film industry, independent of Hollywood.

Korda's commercial instinct told him that the best way to attract American audiences and exhibitors was to delve into British history and serve up a racy version of royal bedroom antics for their titillation. There were two English monarchs that would have been heard of, even in Idaho or South Dakota: Henry VIII and Elizabeth I. With Charles Laughton under contract at the time, it presumably made sense to choose the former, and he dispensed with any serious historical representation, concentrating instead on the dissolute tyrant's shenanigans with his six wives (actually five in the movie itself because a prologue dismisses Henry's first wife as being too respectable to be included in this romp). For the time, it seemed quite steamy, although very tame indeed by today's standards. For example, Laughton as Henry, when approaching his nuptials to the supposedly ugly Anne of Cleves (played by Laughton's wife, Elsa Lanchester) intones, 'The things I do for England!' Lines like these make the film teeter on the edge of being a 1930s version of *Carry On Henry*.

However, what makes the movie of lasting interest are the performances of the leading players (especially Laughton and Lanchester) and the art direction of Korda's brother, Vincent. Shot for a paltry £60,000, both Kordas (as director and art director) managed to make the movie look much more sumptuous. As a screen actor Laughton divides opinion: some see him as a scenery-chewing, megalomaniac old ham, out to dominate any scene he appeared in. Others see him as an actor of genius with extravagant and larger-than-life gifts. He was only 33 when he took on this role and his performance is undoubtedly hammy, but once you reconcile yourself to this style and the overall rumbustious, dig-in-the-ribs tone of the piece, his performance and the movie as a whole become more than merely acceptable entertainment. As history it is bunk. As a movie it is significant in terms of the development of the British film industry and Alexander Korda's role within it.

The 39 Steps (1935)

Crew: directed by Alfred Hitchcock; produced by Michael Balcon and Ivor Montagu; screenplay by Charles Bennett, Alma Reville and Ian Hay (based on the novel by John Buchan); cinematography by Bernard Knowles; music by Louis Levy; edited by Jack Twist. B&W. 85 mins.

Cast: Robert Donat (Richard Hannay); Madeleine Carroll (Pamela); Lucie Mannheim (Miss Smith/Anabella); Godfrey Tearle (Professor Jordan); Peggy Ashcroft (Margaret); John Laurie (John); Helen Haye (Mrs Jordan); Wylie Watson (Mr Memory).

This is probably the best Hitchcock film of his British period. It lacks the depth or darkness of his best Hollywood movies (*Vertigo*, *Notorious*), but is an expertly-produced spy and chase movie that has much more substance than most in the genre. The film from Hitchcock's Hollywood output that it most resembles is *North by Northwest*. Both movies have the male protagonist wrongly accused of murder, forced to flee across country in an attempt to track down the mystery at the centre of the plot. Both encounter rather cool blondes whose motivations are ambiguous. In both, the comfortable, perhaps complacent, world of the hero is overturned and he is forced to behave like a fugitive criminal in order to prove his innocence and restore the normality of his life. *The 39 Steps* and *North by Northwest* are outstanding examples of the paranoid thriller that Hitchcock was such a master at directing.

The story (which differs hugely from the original novel by John Buchan) concerns Richard Hannay, who meets a mysterious woman who tells him about a spy ring that is planning some kind of mayhem. She mentions something about 'the 39 steps' and circles a town on a map of Scotland. When she is murdered, Hannay becomes a wanted man and flees to Scotland to try to track down the leader of the spy ring and amass evidence that will clear him. On the way, he meets Pamela, whom he handcuffs to his person and forces to accompany him. Eventually, he encounters the villainous spies whose aim is to steal a formula to make silent aircraft engines. There is a rousing climax involving a stage memory man with much effective cutting to increase tension.

Hitchcock has a great deal of fun with his hero and heroine handcuffed together, and the overtones of sexual perversity are prominent. Part of Hitchcockian mythology is the story that the director deliberately arranged to have the handcuff keys mislaid on the first day so that his stars were manacled together all day. Robert Donat and Madeleine Carroll play off each other well, although Donat is too ethereal a figure to bring out the full potential of the sexual frisson between the two. Darker overtones are added in a strange scene in a Scottish croft with a young Peggy Ashcroft playing an oppressed wife to John Laurie's puritanical and paranoid husband. Set pieces involve the hero hanging onto to a speeding train crossing the Firth of Forth

railway bridge, a prolonged chase across the Scottish moors
and the final climax in the theatre. The editing of the film
makes effective use of sound, for example, when a
screaming woman changes into the sound of a screeching
train whistle.

The 39 Steps was adapted from a Boys' Own yarn and
given a certain depth and darkness by Hitchcock, so that it
works on both the adventure/spy genre movie level and as
an adult entertainment. Once again, as in Blackmail,
Hitchcock pushes back the boundaries of popular entertainment, inviting audiences to enjoy his film on more than
one level, proving himself both as the so-called 'master of
suspense' and as the director of films that treat the audience
as adults. The movie made international stars of Donat and
Carroll. Hitchcock appeared in almost all of his movies: in
this one, he can be glimpsed throwing some litter as Donat
and Carroll run from the music hall.

Things to Come (1936)

Crew: directed by William Cameron Menzies; produced
by Alexander Korda; screenplay by H.G. Wells and Lajos
Biro adapted from The Shape of Things to Come by H.G.
Wells; cinematography by Georges Perinal; edited by
Charles Crichton and Francis Lyon; music by Arthur Bliss;
production design by Vincent Korda. B&W. 113 mins.

Cast: Raymond Massey (John Cabal/Oswald Cabal);
Edward Chapman (Pippa Passworthy/Raymond Pass-
worthy); Ralph Richardson (The Boss); Margaretta Scott
(Roxana/Rowena); Cedric Hardwicke (Theotocopulos);
Derrick De Marney (Richard Gordon); Ann Todd (Mary
Gordon).

Despite its flaws, *Things to Come* is a testament to the ambition of producer Alexander Korda to make Britain a film-making country of the first rank. He assembled an impressive array of talents to adapt H.G. Wells' 1933 book to the screen: director William Cameron Menzies was a distinguished art director who had worked in Hollywood on the silent versions of *Robin Hood* and *The Thief of Baghdad*; the music was in the hands of Arthur Bliss whose film score was one of the first to be recorded commercially; Wells himself co-wrote the screenplay with Lajos Biro; George Perinal was in charge of photography and Korda's brother designed the entire epic production. Wells later admitted he knew little about writing for the cinema and this is reflected in the film, with its static scenes, its speechi-fying and verbosity and its lack of emotional involvement, but the result is impressive to look at and, at the very least, attempts to deal with important themes of science and progress, technology versus art, war and peace.

The story spans a period of almost a hundred years, beginning in 1940. The fear of impending European war at the time of the production is reflected in Wells' story about Everytown, a metropolis that is almost destroyed by enemy bombers. Years pass and disease has gripped the population, wiping out half of the people of the world. A kind of warlord, The Boss rules Everytown until his brutal authority is challenged by an emissary of 'Wings Over the World', an organisation devoted to rebuilding the world through technology. Faced with the opposition of the present powers-that-be, the organisation that the emissary represents disempowers the citizens of Everytown with the 'gas of peace'. The reconstruction takes place with the city built underground and the use of artificial sunlight. Fast-forward to 2036 and the rulers have decided to colonise the moon, but against the opposition of those who believe that technology has destroyed human values. The wreckers attack the giant space cannon that has been constructed, but the spacecraft is successfully launched.

At times the film resembles a pageant or an illustrated lecture as Wells hammers home his message. Yet Korda's impressive designs are worth seeing, and Raymond Massey and Cedric Harwicke manage creditable performances amongst all the empty rhetoric. The cost of the movie ($1.5 million, a very large sum for that time) does show on screen. This is large-scale movie spectacle for a mass audience with a moralising, Wellesian message thrown in for their betterment.

Things to Come is an oddity of British film history. Korda undoubtedly took a risk in producing it and initially it seemed the film would be a box-office flop, but it gradually acquired a cult reputation. It remains one of the most interesting British movies of the decade and evidence that the industry was taking itself seriously.

The Lady Vanishes (1938)

Crew: directed by Alfred Hitchcock; produced by Edward Black; screenplay by Sidney Gilliat and Frank Launder, adapted from the novel *The Wheel Spins* by Ethel Lina White; cinematography by Jack Cox; edited by Alfred Roome; music by Louis Levy. B&W. 97 mins.

Cast: Margaret Lockwood (Iris Henderson); Michael Redgrave (Gilbert Redman); Paul Lukas (Dr Hartz); Dame May Whitty (Miss Froy); Cecil Parker (Eric Todhunter); Linden Travers (Margaret Todhunter); Mary Clare (Baroness); Naunton Wayne (Caldicott); Basil Radford (Charters).

This movie is a highpoint for those Hitchcock admirers who prefer his early British phase to his later Hollywood output. In fact, Hitchcock was only a last-minute substitute as director, but once aboard, he licked the script into Hitchcockian shape with the help of his wife, Alma Reville, and Launder and Gilliat who would later become stalwarts of the British movie scene as co-writers of movies such as *Kipps*, *Night Train to Munich*, *The Happiest Days of Your Life* and the St Trinians series. *The Lady Vanishes* sits firmly in the tradition of the genteel English detective story à la Agatha Christie and Dorothy L Sayers. Hollywood, by contrast, would allow him to explore the underbelly of the human condition in shockers such as *Psycho* and *Vertigo*.

The story mainly takes place aboard a train travelling towards England through Central Europe. A rather dotty old woman disappears on board and a young woman (Lockwood) who has befriended her sets out to discover what has happened, aided by a bow-tied music scholar (Redgrave). The villains are very villainous and clearly intended to represent malevolent German Nazis the film was made a year before the start of the Second World War). Caldicott and Charters, two very upper-class Englishmen who are obsessed with the latest score in the Test Match, are also on the train. The old woman turns out to be a courageous spy of sorts, in possession of vital information that must be passed onto the British authorities. After much suspense and danger, the decent British defeat the baddies and she is restored to life.

Never taking itself too seriously, *The Lady Vanishes* still incorporates some genuinely sinister aspects. A criticism that could be levelled at it is a tendency towards xenophobia: the British are portrayed as relentlessly eccentric but decent, while most foreigners are either downright nasty or stupid. In that rather reprehensible light, the movie enters into the 'little Englander' world of Agatha Christie and other writers of English detective fiction. However, it touched on an immediate pre-war paranoia about Germans in particular and Europe in general, and a sub-text of the movie certainly seems to be that it is rather dangerous to leave British shores and mix with Johnny Foreigner. This attitude is personified in the characters played by Basil Radford and Naunton Wayne, the obsessive cricket fans: depending on your point of view, an endearing national characteristic or a complacent, class-based irritation.

The Lady Vanishes was a huge success on both sides of the Atlantic and is viewed by Hitchcockian devotees as one of his major works. It is an interesting period piece from a director who would go on to produce far finer work in Hollywood. Hitchcock can be seen in the scene set at Victoria Station near the end of the movie.

The Four Feathers (1939)

Crew: directed by Zoltan Korda; produced by Alexander Korda; screenplay by RC Sherriff, Lajos Biro and Arthur Wimperis, adapted from the novel by AEW Mason; cinematography by Georges Perinal, Osmond Borrodaille and Jack Cardiff; music by Miklos Rozsa; edited by William Hornbeck and Henry Cornelius; production design by Vincent Korda. Colour. 130 mins.

Cast: John Clements (Harry Faversham); Ralph Richardson (Captain John Durrance); C Aubrey Smith (General Burroughs); June Duprez (Ethne Burroughs); Allan Jeayes (General Faversham); Jack Allen (Lieutenant Willoughby); Donald Gray (Peter Burroughs).

This epic movie, adapted from a 1902 novel by AEW Mason, is a definite landmark of British cinema. It celebrates the British Empire and the traditions of the British military class in a generally unembarrassed way. Made just before the onset of World War Two, it is a rallying call to the colours; any doubts raised about militarism and imperialism are shrouded in the overall glorification of British military might and courage.

The story concerns Harry Faversham who, coming from a distinguished army family, decides to resign his commission on the eve of leaving with his regiment to fight in the Sudan wars of 1889. He is branded a coward by his three closest friends and his fiancé who send him a white feather each, hence the title of the movie. However, to prove that his courage is not in doubt, Faversham leaves for the Sudan where he disguises himself as a native and pretends to belong to the Sengali tribe and to have had his tongue cut off. There he witnesses the massacre of a British army unit, but manages to rescue one of his friends who has been blinded by overlong exposure to the desert sun. He then intervenes dramatically in freeing British prisoners from a jail, an action that helps the British forces to an overwhelming victory over the massed 'Fuzzi Wuzzies'. On his return from the Sudan, his friends take back their feathers and his fiancée asks for his forgiveness. The lad has proved himself a good brick after all.

The Four Feathers is another Boys' Own yarn dedicated to the glory of war and empire. Whatever questions it seems to raise about the unreasonable demands that a gung-ho military career may make on an individual are swept aside as the tale of adventure and daring unfolds. There is no whiff of doubt about the right of Britain to be in Egypt and the Sudan as an imperialistic power. Some old army generals are lampooned for their outrageous posturing, but this is minor compared to the narrative imperative for the hero to prove himself a hero in the eyes of his comrades and the country.

What is impressive about the film is the scale of the battle scenes, which have been recycled on numerous occasions in other films . The desert milieu is used with tremendous effect and the thousands of local extras employed to represent the massed armies of the native populations add an authentic impression of the terror of warfare. The use of technicolor is equally impressive. Although Clements is rather stiff as the lead, Ralph Richardson gives an outstanding performance as the hero's blinded officer friend. The schoolboy heroics teeter on the brink of risibility, for example, when the disguised hero produces a flute to play in front of the cage where his erstwhile friends are imprisoned, along the side of which he has written 'Do not despair!'. There is no doubt that, viewed from today's perspective, there are strong racist overtones to the movie; subsequent versions of this tale have played down this element. Yet it is a major film in the history of the British cinema and was a huge success internationally.

Other Notable British Films of this Period

The Lodger (1926)
The Man Who Knew Too Much (1934)
Rembrandt (1936)
Night Mail (1936)
Fire Over England (1936)
Sabotage (1936)
Secret Agent (1936)
The Edge of the World (1937)

GREAT BRITISH MOVIES

Bank Holiday (1938)
The Stars Look Down (1939)
Jamaica Inn (1939)

The Golden Age of British Cinema:
1940–49

The Second World War saw a surge in the numbers of
people going to the cinema on both sides of the Atlantic,
and the peak year for attendances was 1946. Thereafter,
with the advent of television sets in almost every home and
changes to the Hollywood studio structure, audiences
declined by around half in the next decade, both here and
in the USA. Nevertheless, the wartime boom coincided
with a number of memorable British films and this trend
was extended into the immediate post-war era before the
decline of the 1950s. The domestic film industry was at last
a rival to Hollywood and home-grown stars such as James
Mason, Stewart Granger, Margaret Lockwood, Anna
Neagle, Trevor Howard, John Mills, Laurence Olivier,
Gracie Fields and Patricia Roc topped popularity polls
with British cinemagoers, whilst directors such as Carol
Reed, Michael Powell, Laurence Olivier and David Lean
became recognisable names to the public and ensured
quality. The Rank Organisation, and its subsidiary
Gainsborough Pictures, dominated production and distri-
bution, and many of their films, such as *The Wicked Lady*
and *The Seventh Veil*, outgrossed top Hollywood movies.
Ealing Studios, however, under the stewardship of Michael
Balcon, forged an independent path, producing numerous
films of lasting quality, especially comedies. Alexander

Korda and his London Films continued to make movies of significance.

In the wartime and the immediate post-war years, British filmmakers supposed that audiences would be seeking escapist entertainment and this was largely what Gainsborough Studios served up with great success, in the cinematic equivalent of literary bodice-rippers. Gainsborough specialised in period melodramas, where the frocks were almost as important as the storylines. Films such as *The Man in Grey*, which shot Stewart Granger to stardom, *Jassy* with the ever-present Margaret Lockwood, *Madonna of the Seven Moons*, *The Wicked Lady*, a preposterous tale of highwaymen and women, and *Blanche Fury*, had audiences queuing around the block. The war itself was represented in numerous sturdy and propagandist movies such as *In Which We Serve*, a shameless hymn of praise to the officer class, *Above Us the Waves*, *The Way to the Stars* and a whole raft of others. The documentary tradition found a new star in the films of Humphrey Jennings, including *London Can Take It* and *Fires Were Started*. Comedy, a means of distancing the grimness of war and its aftermath, was served up in movies starring George Formby, Sid Field, Alistair Sim and the Crazy Gang, most of which, but not all, were entirely forgettable. British movies, never strong on musicals, hit box-office bonanzas with the Anna Neagle/Michael Wilding pairing in *Maytime in Mayfair* and *Spring in Park Lane*, artificial glimpses of life among the rich and the aristocratic for the mass audience to consume.

Any choice of top British films of this decade is necessarily partial and personal, as there are more films competing for inclusion that can be accommodated. A few, such as *The Seventh Veil* and *The Way to the Stars*, are included not only for their intrinsic worth, but also because

they are representative of their genre, the melodrama and
the war movie respectively. Sadly in some ways, the 1940s
marked a peak for British cinema, not only in terms of
commercial success but also for artistic merit. It would be
comforting to think that an indigenous film industry could
once again match this success, but this seems unlikely.

The Thief of Baghdad (1940)

Crew: directed by Ludwig Berger, Michael Powell, Tim
Whelan, Zoltan Korda, William Cameron Menzies,
Alexander Korda; produced by Alexander Korda; screenplay
by Lajos Biro and Miles Malleson; cinematography by
Georges Perinal and Osmond Borrodaille; music by Miklos
Rozsa; edited by William Hornbeck; production by Vincent
Korda; special effects by Lawrence Butler, Tom Howard and
John Mills; costumes by Oliver Messel, John Armstrong and
Marcel Vertes. Colour. 106 mins.

Cast: Conrad Veidt (Jaffar); Sabu (Abu); June Duprez
(Princess); John Justin (Ahmad); Rex Ingram (Djinni);
Miles Malleson (The Sultan); Morton Selten (The King);
Mary Morris (Halima).

British movies, whatever else they may be, have always
enjoyed the reputation of possessing high production
values, technical expertise and aesthetic taste, and *The Thief
of Baghdad* is testament to the talents of British technicians
and specialists in all the cinematic arts. Essentially, the
movie is an outrageously camp piece of Arabian Nights
fantasy, an over-rich, ersatz 'Orientalist' dish served up for
Western palates. However, if you can stomach its whimsy,
its representation of Arab stereotypes (thieves, wicked

magicians, harems, magic carpets and so on) and its essential juvenility, the movie is a delight to the eye and amusing for its naivety.

The story is more or less an excuse for lots of colourful sets and costumes and the use of extravagant (for its day) special effects. Sabu plays Abu, a street urchin living by his wits and thieving, who is thrown into a Baghdad jail where he encounters the deposed ruler, Prince Ahmad. The evil Grand Vizzier, Jaffar, is the number one villain (played by the striking Conrad Veidt) who has designs on the Princess, whom Ahmad, once he has escaped with Abu, falls in love with. Jaffar, who has amazing magical powers, turns Ahmad into a blind beggar and Abu into a dog. The Princess, resisting a fate worse than death, agrees to marry Jaffar if he will lift the curse. Eventually, good triumphs with the help of a genie (Rex Ingram), and order, as in all good fairy tales, is restored. Abu leaves waving to all from the magic carpet.

What stays with you is the use of technicolor, the imaginative fantasy sets and the effects, such as the magic carpet and the genie, the musical score by Miklos Rosza and the film's successful creation of a never-never land of unending childhood. Five directors shared the directing credits including the most talented of them, Michael Powell, who would go on to direct some of the most interesting British movies of this golden age. The Korda brothers, Alexander, Zoltan and Vincent, played a huge part in bringing this project to fruition. Lawrence Butler and Jack Whitney won the 1940 Oscar® for Special Effects for their work. Conrad Veidt added menace to the proceedings and Sabu was suddenly elevated to star status.

The film has always been much admired by the 'movie brats' generation; directors such as Coppola, Scorsese and Lucas regularly pay tribute to it and the subsequent films directed by Michael Powell. It remains an oddity, however, a product of its time. Some of its special effects may well seem rather amateurish to those brought up on *Star Wars*, but it certainly has infinitely more innate charm than any of the six movies of that series. As Britain faced up to a long war of attrition at home and abroad, *The Thief of Baghdad* was just the kind of fantastic extravaganza needed to replace harsh reality with gossamer unreality.

The Life and Death of Colonel Blimp (1943)

Crew: directed by Michael Powell; produced by Michael Powell and Emeric Pressburger; screenplay by Michael Powell and Emeric Pressburger; cinematography by Jack Cardiff and Georges Perinal; music by Allan Gray; edited by John Seabourne. Colour. 163 mins.

Cast: Roger Livesey (Clive Candy); Deborah Kerr (Edith Hunter/Barbara Wynee/Johnny Cannon); Anton Walbrook (Theo Kretschmar-Schuldorff); Roland Culver (Colonel Betteridge); Albert Lieven (Von Ritter); John Laurie (Murdoch).

This is certainly the oddest of British war movies, but none the worse for that, possessed as it is with a complexity and ambiguity that other examples of the genre almost invariably lack. It was the first film that Powell and Pressburger produced for their new production company, The Archers, and was loosely based on a character created by cartoonist Low for the *Daily Express* newspaper. Blimp symbolised the old officer class who were hidebound, right-wing and militarily out-of-date, and whose grip over the military machine might lose Britain the war. Winston Churchill objected to the portrayal of the officer class as bumbling reactionaries and put pressure on Laurence Olivier, who was marked for the role, to turn it down on the basis that the movie would be bad for morale. Olivier did indeed turn the part down and the admirable Roger Livesey took over.

The action spans the years between 1902 and 1943. Clive Candy has won a VC for his heroics in the Boer War and goes to Germany to trap a German spy. He makes friends with a fiercely proud German officer, Theo, after they have fought a duel over accusations that the British had mistreated the Boers during the Boer war. Theo steals the young woman whom Candy is hoping to marry. However, Theo meets another young woman during the First World War who reminds him of his first love so he marries her. Flash-forward to the Second World War and Candy's wife has died and Theo has become a refugee from Hitler's Germany. Now an old buffoon, Candy's old-fashioned views and military strategies are exposed as irrelevant to the needs of modern warfare.

Winston Churchill forbade the exporting of *Blimp* for two years because he believed it represented the wrong image of the British war effort. In fact, Powell and Pressburger have a definite propagandist agenda in the film: the old officer class have to be replaced by thrusting imaginative young officers who realise what total war means. That said, the Blimp character, although sidelined in his old age and shown to be redundant, is dealt with sympathetically, as is his aristocratic German friend, which is a tribute to the filmmakers considering that in the war years most Germans were demonised as the Nazi enemy.

The Powell and Pressburger eccentricity is well to the fore and the film, shot in technicolor, is, as usual with their films, never less than beguiling to look at. Livesey is terrific as Candy, Deborah Kerr is perfect in three roles and Anton Walbrook as the German resists his natural tendency to chew the scenery to deliver a fine performance. The film is about war only in part: it is also about love, friendship, nationality, dreams and ambitions, chivalry and ethical values. Despite its rambling structure, the movie stands high in the canon of Powell and Pressburger, and deserves consideration as one of the best British films ever made

Henry V (1944)

Crew: directed by Laurence Olivier; produced by Olivier and Filippo Del Guidice; screenplay by Alan Dent and Olivier based on the play by William Shakespeare; cinematography by Robert Krasker; music by William Walton; edited by Reginald Beck; art direction by Paul Sheriff; costumes by Roger Furse. Colour. 127 mins.

Cast: Laurence Olivier (Henry V); Robert Newton (Pistol); Leslie Banks (Chorus); Renee Asherson (Princess Katherine); Esmond Knight (Fluellen); Leo Genn (Constable of France); Felix Aylmer (Archbishop of Canterbury); Ralph Truman (Mountjoy); Harcourt Williams (King Charles).

It is not difficult to understand why Shakespeare's play about a warlike Henry the Fifth should be considered extremely relevant to a Britain at war with Hitler's Germany, Mussolini's Italy and Japan. Olivier himself, fiercely and perhaps naively patriotic, was more than eager to do his bit on screen, albeit he was already serving in an inglorious role in the navy. The play has an unpleasant jingoistic tone, which doubtless reflected the prevalent political situation in Elizabethan times. In the depths of war, however, this jingoism was perceived as a rousing call to arms and a glorification of British values and courage.

Olivier and co-adaptor Alan Dent had the marvellous idea of the opening section, which represents a performance of the play as it would have been performed in Shakespeare's Globe Theatre itself on the South Bank of the Thames in London. Thereafter it moves away from the theatre to the royal court and then to France, Agincourt and then back to the Globe. This structure reminds us of the theatrical origins of the source material, but it also manages to be resoundingly cinematic as well.

Overall, the film is a triumph for Olivier as actor, director, producer and adaptor. His performance as Henry cannot be surpassed and his vocal range has never been better employed. He makes a believably heroic figure and his St Crispin's Day speech before the battle of Agincourt is a stirring aria sending a straightforward message of defiance and guts in the face of adversity to the British people. Olivier lost the 1946 Oscar® to Frederic March for his performance in *The Best Years of Our Lives*, but was compensated with a Special Award Oscar®. Olivier had a special talent as a director for filming Shakespeare because of his experience as a classical actor and stage director, and the fact that he had learnt cinematic craft from Hollywood directors such as Hitchcock and William Wyler. In addition, he had the good sense to surround himself with some top film people, including Reginald Beck (who directed when Olivier was in front of the cameras), Robert Krasker, a great lighting cameraman, and Paul Sheriff, who did wonders on a limited budget on the sets as did Roger Furse on costumes. The colour is splendid, perhaps too splendid, if

the gruesome reality of what war must have been like in
the fifteenth century is taken into account, but the film's
purpose is the glorification of the war effort, not to present
a realistic picture of the cost of war. The Battle of Agincourt
is staged as a thrilling pageant with stirring music by Walton
and with the camera moving with the English knights on
horseback as they charge the French defences.

Any faults the movie has belong to the original play: the
rather tiresome comic interplay among the lower orders, for
example, and some static scenes in which Henry tries to find
legal justification for the war. The Globe scenes, however, are
a triumph and clearly staged by people with a real understanding of what Shakespeare's Globe must have been like.

The Way to the Stars (1945)

Crew: directed by Anthony Asquith; produced by Anatole
de Grunwald; screenplay by Ternece Rattigan and Anatole
de Grunwald with the poem *Johnny in the Sky* written by
John Pudney; cinematography by Derrick Williams; music
by Nicholas Brodszky. B&W. 109 mins.

Cast: John Mills (Peter Penrose); Rosamund John (Miss
Todd); Michael Redgrave (David Archdale); Douglass
Montgomery (Johnny Hollis); Basil Radford (Tiny
Williams); Stanley Holloway (Mr Palmer); Joyce Carey
(Miss Winterton); Renee Asherson (Iris Winterton); Felix
Aylmer (Rev. Charles Moss); Bonar Colleano (Joe Frizelli);
Trevor Howard (Squadron-Leader Carter); Jean Simmons
(A Singer).

This is one of the more thoughtful of British war movies,
largely due to Rattigan's script, which explored the

emotions and dreams of a group of RAF and American airmen in the latter years of the conflict. Its tone is stiff upper-lip; and yet again it is a hymn to the officer class, with the working class, as usual, granted only walk-on status. John Pudney wrote two poems for the movie and one of them, *Johnny in the Sky*, became much quoted, partly because it seemed to make a comment about social reform and the debt the country would owe those who had sacrificed their lives:

> Fetch out no shroud
> For Johnny-in-the-cloud;
> And keep your tears
> For him in after years.
> Better by far,
> For Johnny – the bright star,
> To keep your head
> And see his children fed.

In his stage plays (*The Winslow Boy*, *The Browning Version*, *The Deep Blue Sea*) and screenplays, Rattigan generally seemed to take a liberal Tory stance: he belonged to the upper middle-class himself and represented that class on stage, but was not uncritical of their smugness and their privileged place in society. However, in this film he represented the officer class as mainly 'good eggs', courageously trying to do their best to win the war for an England they love. *The Way to the Stars* is not a gung-ho movie and there are relatively few air battle sequences. Anthony Asquith would later direct the screen version of Rattigan's stage play, *The Winslow Boy* and also a celebrated version of Wilde's *The Importance of Being Earnest*. He was never an innovative or challenging director, but he could be depended on to turn in a well-made, literate movie, with good performances and middlebrow themes handled with some sensitivity.

The Way to the Stars is certainly one of the best of British war movies and interesting historically for it looks beyond the war itself to peacetime and the changes that need to be made in British society. Another noteworthy feature of the movie is that it marked the debut of two actors who would reach international film stardom status in later years: Jean Simmons and Trevor Howard. At the heart of the film, however, are those two most English of actors, John Mills and Michael Redgrave. Mills appeared in so many war movies that he became an icon of British grit and resistance to the Nazi war machine. He was a reassuringly steadfast and decent figure, and the message seemed to be that as long as the country had Johnny Mills fighting for us, then all would be well.

Brief Encounter (1945)

Crew: directed by David Lean; produced by Noel Coward; screenplay by Noel Coward, David Lean and Anthony Havelock-Allan, based on the play *Still Life* by Noel Coward; cinematography by Robert Krasker; edited by Jack Harris. B&W. 86 mins.

Cast: Celia Johnson (Laura Jesson); Trevor Howard (Alec Harvey); Cyril Raymond (Fred Jesson); Stanley Holloway (Albert Godby); Joyce Carey (Myrtle Bagot); Everley Gregg (Dolly Messiter).

The story of a very British middle-class near-love affair played to the strains of Rachmaninov's Second Piano

Concerto, *Brief Encounter*, despite its sometimes ludicrous representation of the timidities and repressions of the lovers, has acquired an almost iconic reputation over the years. A worthy doctor and a suburban wife bump into each other in town one day and they begin seeing each other clandestinely. However, this being the mid-1940s and the characters being English, the affair is not consummated; the lovers part at the end of the movie, the man destined for a medical job in Africa, the woman doomed to her unexciting marriage with a dull husband. Despite its restraints, the film touched a nerve among the cinema-going public in its exploration of repressed longings and the desire to escape middle-class respectability.

The class divisions of England, as seen through the eyes of Coward and Lean, are rigid: the upper middle-class characters (the Celia Johnson character has a cook and a maid) are portrayed as polite and refined, whilst the lower orders they encounter in the station cafe are seen as comical and mock-genteel. Viewed from a vantage point 60 years later, the film portrays an immediate post-war Britain where social mobility seems unlikely, although there are hints that the working classes are becoming restless. Robert Krasker's photography is one of the best features of the movie, especially the moody, neo-realist scenes in the railway station (shot partly at Carnforth in Yorkshire).

Brief Encounter is meant to be a tear-jerker, as the heavy use of Rachmaninov on the soundtrack signals, yet it is hard to deny the effectiveness of the underscoring, and there is a real sense of doomed hopes in this tale of suburban love. Celia Johnson is at her most effective in this role and Trevor Howard became a star after this movie. *Brief Encounter* deserves its place because of the sheer professionalism of its makers and because, for all its faults, it remains one of the most evocative of British movies through its representation of a bygone Britain.

The Seventh Veil (1946)

Crew: directed by Compton Bennett; produced by Sidney Box; screenplay by Muriel and Sidney Box; cinematography by Reginald Wyer; music by Benjamin Frankel; edited by Gordon Hales; art direction by James Carter. B&W. 95 mins.

Cast: James Mason (Nicholas); Ann Todd (Francesca Cunningham); Herbert Lom (Dr Larson); Hugh McDermott (Peter Gay); Albert Lieven (Maxwell Lewyden); Yvonne Owen (Susan Brook); David Horne (Dr Kendal).

This film was a huge hit in Britain and enjoyed considerable success in America as well, with the Boxes winning the Original Screenplay Oscar® for their efforts. It is a strange sado-masochistic tale with James Mason again playing a moody, unpleasant anti-hero whom audiences loved to hate. However, this kind of role, which he began to detest, did his box-office standing no harm at all, as he was regularly voted the top British male star in annual polls.

The film is largely told in flashback, a characteristic of film noir, which this film resembles. Film noir also often deals with psychoanalysis and mental illness, both prominent elements of this story. Francesca is a distinguished pianist who suffers from bouts of severe depression and who attempts to kill herself. Dr Larson, a psychiatrist, endeavours to unravel the causes of her illness. Nicholas is her guardian; sadistic towards her and fiercely possessive; he objects to her relationships with men on the grounds that such distractions would harm her art, but he is clearly struggling with his own feelings for her. He crashes a car with Francesca in it and her hands are burnt, but she recovers her ability to play and the ending of the film sees her returning to her guardian and the strong implication is that they will end up together as lovers.

Overtones of incest, sado-masochism, sexual guilt and repression make for a heady melodramatic brew. The film-makers were uncertain about how to end the film and consulted preview audiences, who voted that Todd should end up with Mason. Considering that he has done his best to harm her in the car incident and in another scene, where he almost bangs the piano lid down on her hands, it seems as though the audience were opting for perversity over normality. However, because James Mason was playing the part, they clearly wanted the heroine to be rewarded with his love at the end of the movie.

The film's treatment of psychiatry and mental illness is perhaps risibly superficial in the same way that many Hollywood movies of the same era were. Melodrama, how-ever, does not deal in realism, its driving force is emotion and violence, and there are plenty of both in *The Seventh Veil*. Why the film was such a huge hit at the time might be difficult to gauge now, but Mason's popularity had much to do with it. The piece could be saying something about gender relations of the period and the oppression of women, some of whom take refuge in madness; at the end, the film awards the male oppressor with the victory.

Great Expectations (1946)

Crew: directed by David Lean; produced by Ronald Neame; screenplay by David Lean, Ronald Neame,

Anthony Havelock-Allen, Cecil McGivern, Kay Walsh, based on the novel by Charles Dickens; cinematography by Guy Green; edited by Jack Harris; music by Walter Goehr; production design by John Bryan. B&W. 118 mins.

Cast: John Mills (Pip); Valerie Hobson (Estella); Bernard Miles (Joe Gargery); Francis L Sullivan (Jaggers); Martita Hunt (Miss Havisham); Finlay Currie (Abel Magwitch); Anthony Wager (Pip as a child); Jean Simmons (Estella as a child); Alec Guinness (Herbert Pocket).

This is perhaps director David Lean's finest film, although he is best known for epics such as *The Bridge on the River Kwai*, *Lawrence of Arabia* and *Doctor Zhivago*. The director and other key personnel bring a sure hand to adapting Dickens' classic Victorian novel to the screen and there are only a few false notes in the film. The casting, for example, is not perfect: John Mills was 38 by the time he made this movie and it is stretching the audience's credulity to accept him as a young and naive Pip arriving in London for the first time.

The early scenes of the film set in the Essex marshes are the most memorable: Pip, the local blacksmith's son, helps an escaped convict, who is eventually recaptured. When he reaches young adulthood, Pip receives a legacy, which allows him to lead a fashionable life in London. He wrongly thinks the money has come from Miss Havisham, a man-hating recluse, who has introduced him to her ward for the purpose of breaking his heart just as hers was broken when she was jilted on her wedding day. Eventually, Pip in his pride learns that his benefactor was the convict whom he had helped all those years ago. He learns some humility and recovers his humanity in trying to save the convict's life.

Other memorable scenes are set in the decaying surroundings of Miss Havisham's mansion. Here John Bryan's designs and the art direction by Wilfred Shingleton are at their finest. Francis L Sullivan, Martita Hunt and Finlay Currie are excellent in supporting roles, whilst a young Jean Simmons made an early appearance as the proud and scornful young Estella. Critics of British cinema can point to this kind of literary adaptation as evidence that the British are adept at raiding their literary heritage to furnish subject-matter for their movies rather than creating films from non-literary sources, but when it is done this well, that seems like mere quibbling.

A Matter of Life and Death (1946)

Crew: directed by Michael Powell and Emeric Pressburger; produced by Hein Heckroth; screenplay by Michael Powell and Emeric Pressburger; cinematography by Jack Cardiff; music by Allan Gray; edited by Reginald Mills; production design by Alfred Junge; art direction by Arthur Lawson; costumes by Hein Heckroth. Technicolor. 104 mins.

Cast: David Niven (Carter); Roger Livesey (Dr Reeves); Kim Hunter (June); Marius Goring (Conductor 71); Raymond Massey (Abraham Farlan); Kathleen Byron (An Angel); Richard Attenborough (English Pilot); Bonar Colleano (American Pilot).

This Powell and Pressburger extravaganza deserves its place in cinema history, if only for its ambition and the confidence of its execution. David Niven plays a World War Two airman who is forced to bail out and suffers brain damage.

At the core of the movie is an extended sequence in what purports to be heaven during which the matter of the airman's life or death is debated: whether he should be granted a reprieve because he has fallen in love and because of the error made by heaven. Sundry other issues are debated in a heavenly debating chamber, including love, our responsibilities for one another and what kind of society should be built post-war. No one could claim that the issues are examined with any philosophical weight and in the end the Niven character is restored to life and the love of the control tower WRAF who talked him down when his plane was struck by enemy fire.

It is all rather complacently British public school, but the production values and the colour photography by Jack Cardiff imbue the film with a lasting worth. As a matter of personal taste, I find Niven hard to take in the leading role, his palpable self-satisfaction working against any unease that the screenplay may set up. However, the sheer verve and imagination of the overall concept of the movie sweeps the viewer along, allowing you to forget about its essential silliness and the hollowness of some of the ideas. Style is meaning and never is that credo more apparent and applicable than here. No one else in British movies of this time, or any other time, for that matter, was attempting anything remotely as fantastical or ambitious.

Alfred Junge's production design is outstanding, in particular the gigantic, seemingly limitless stairway to heaven on which the famous of history parade. Jack Cardiff's colour photography is also terrific. Although Powell and Pressburger must take their full share of the credit for the movie's achievements, this surely illustrates what a collaborative medium filmmaking is. *A Matter of Life and Death* can usefully be referred to as a Michael Powell or a Powell–Pressburger movie, but it was the product of many different talents.

Odd Man Out (1946)

Crew: directed by Carol Reed; produced by Carol Reed; screenplay by FL Green and RC Sherriff based on the novel by FL Green; cinematography by Robert Krasker; edited by Fergus McDonell; music by William Alwyn; production design by Roger Furse; art direction by Ralph Brinton. B&W. 116 mins.

Cast: James Mason (Johnny McQueen); Robert Newton (Lukey); Kathleen Ryan (Kathleen); Robert Beatty (Dennis); William Hartnell (Barman); F J McCormick (Shell); Fay Compton (Rosie); Beryl Measor (Maudie); Cyril Cusack (Pat); Dan O'Herlihy (Nolan).

This is surely one of the contenders for the best British film of all time. Even for 1947, its sympathetic portrayal of IRA members was a brave gesture in the face of British hostility. It is difficult to imagine that such a film could be made now starring the leading British star of his day. It is James Mason's finest film and certainly one of director Carol Reed's greatest achievements.

Johnny and his IRA cohort plan a daring robbery of a payroll from a factory, but the heist goes wrong and Johnny accidentally kills a man and is himself seriously wounded while attempting his getaway. Abandoned by the panicky driver of the getaway car, Johnny enters a nightmare world of night-time Belfast where every policeman is on the hunt for him and locals are tempted to hand him over to the authorities for their own gain. He is variously cared for by a scavenger bum, an eccentric painter and two genteel ladies. Meanwhile, his loyal girlfriend is searching for him. The dying Johnny makes one last desperate attempt to reach the docks to escape on a boat but he is surrounded and dies in her arms.

Robert Krasker's photography, William Alwyn's music and Reed's imaginative and sympathetic direction underscore the dark tragedy of the hero's descent into hell and his ultimate death. The audience is invited to forget that they are watching the death throes of an IRA gunman and by the end of the movie the Mason figure has become almost Christ-like in his suffering. Mason brings a depth of feeling to the role that he never bettered. Amazingly, the *Odd Man Out* script was first sent to Stewart Granger, who apparently skimmed through it to see how many lines he had and turned it down because it wasn't large enough a part for a star of his magnitude. We should all be very grateful for that star's ego, because it's hard to think of Granger playing the Mason role without wincing.

Kathleen Ryan is luminous as the gunman's lover and she, like Kathleen Byron, is one of those actresses that the British cinema never made full use of because her looks were not conventionally beautiful enough. Robert Newton gives one of his larger-than-life performances as the artist as crazy man, but somehow such bravura suits the overwrought nature of the drama. Irish actor FJ McCormick is outstanding as the ferrety, would-be Judas torn between his desire for a reward and his better feelings.

A possible criticism of *Odd Man Out* is that it wears its literary origins on its cinematic sleeve and it is true that the ripe characterisations are taken straight from the page of a novel, but Reed manages to dovetail these influences into a portrait of a Belfast on one day that is rich in its detail and authentic in its atmosphere. The film did not perform well at the box-office when it was first released, possibly because of its IRA subject-matter and the hostility of certain newspapers to its representation of IRA members, but over the years it has acquired a reputation that puts it up there with the very best of British movies.

Black Narcissus (1947)

Crew: directed by Michael Powell; produced by Michael Powell and Emeric Pressburger; screenplay by Michael Powell and Emeric Pressburger, based on the novel by Rumer Godden; cinematography by Jack Cardiff; edited by Reginald Mills; music by Brian Easdale. Colour. 100 mins.

Cast: Deborah Kerr (Sister Clodagh); Sabu (Dilip Rai); David Farrar (Mr Dean); Flora Robson (Sister Philippa); Jean Simmons (Kanchi); Esmond Knight (Gen. Toda Rai); Kathleen Byron (Sister Ruth); Jenny Laird (Sister Honey); Judith Furse (Sister Briony).

It is a tribute to British film technicians that *Black Narcissus* is set in the Himalayas in a castle perched among the cloud-capped peaks and almost the whole movie was shot in the studio and still looks wonderful. There are also some ravishing scenes shot in a Sussex garden and some exterior sequences to represent Ireland in flashback sequences. The film deservedly won the Oscars® for colour cinematography and art direction. Adapted from a novel of the same name by Rumer Godden, *Black Narcissus* is an intense melodrama about sex, repression, clash of cultures and Britishness, and for its period is amazingly up-front about the dangers of repressed passions.

A group of nuns are trying to establish a school and a hospital in the local ruler's palace high in the mountains. The palace used to be a harem and its 'ghosts' seem to gradually affect the nuns. Their leader is Sister Clodagh, who is unsure of herself in her new position of authority and is further unsettled by her attraction to the local British government agent, Mr Dean, who is also the target of the repressed instincts of Sister Ruth. Matters come to a climax when Sister Ruth, consumed by her jealousy of Clodagh, tries to kill her but plunges to her own death. The film ends with the nuns departing the region, defeated by their own emotions and the conflicting culture of the locals.

Playing up the melodrama, the director elicits a strong performance from Kathleen Byron as Sister Ruth in particular. One shot of the demented Byron, by then dressed in contemporary clothes and flaunting lurid lipstick, as she appears through a doorway and approaches with murderous intent the figure of the Mother Superior, is as chilling as any Hitchcock ever directed. Despite her success in this film, Byron's career never really took off, perhaps because she was not seen as 'beautiful' enough. Deborah Kerr had no such problems, but she also delivers a subtle performance as the tormented Mother Superior. David Farrar in his shorts and with his pipe-smoking persona seems an unlikely target for such unrequited passion, but then isolation in the Himalayas is likely to induce erratic behaviour. Sabu, the Indian-born young star of numerous British movies of the 1940s, is a prince in love with a peasant girl played by Jean Simmons ('browning up' for the role).

Emeric and Pressburger were British film-makers attempting to deal with 'daring' subject-matter, and in doing so use all the cinematic arts in ways that others in the British industry would never have been able to attempt. Sometimes, their films border on becoming risible and camp; they have a beguiling 'silliness' to them, but that is part of their charm, just as it is with the melodramas directed by Douglas Sirk in 1950s Hollywood. Nevertheless, despite their foibles and their occasional preciousness, these Powell and Pressburger movies have a lasting quality that influenced later generations of moviemakers.

It Always Rains on Sundays (1947)

Crew: directed by Robert Hamer; produced by Henry Cornelius; screenplay by Angus Macphail, Robert Hamer and Henry Cornelius, from a novel by Arthur La Bern; cinematography by Douglas Slocombe; music by Georges Auric. B&W. 92 mins.

Cast: Googie Withers (Rose); John McCallum (Tommy Swann); Jack Warner (Fothergill); Edward Chapman (George Sandigate), Susan Shaw (Vi), Patricia Punket (Doris); Sydney Tafler (Lou Hyams); Jimmy Hanley (Whitey).

This classic British movie was an Ealing Studio production and is untypical of their output in its gritty realism and the working-class milieu of London's East End. The Italians at this time were making neo-realist movies such as *Bicycle Thieves* and *Rome. Open City*; *It Always Rains on Sundays* is an attempt at neo-realism and for once in the British cinema of its time, working-class characters are portrayed sympathetically and unsentimentally, and not used for comic effect.

The action takes place during one Sunday in an area of the East End close to a market, obviously intended to be

Petticoat Lane. Once again, as in *Brief Encounter*, a wife is trapped in domesticity and married to a decent but dull husband. Suddenly, a lover from her past turns up in her home; he is an escaped criminal and the police are after him. Their earlier passion is rekindled, but he is killed while trying to escape. The wife is destined to resume her life of drudgery and routine. Her step-daughter, played by Susan Shaw, also dreams of escape as well and becomes involved with a married man, whilst the other daughter in the family falls out with her boyfriend and then makes up with him, presaging the fact that she is destined for the same kind of life as her mother. The title of the movie reflects the melancholy of its viewpoint: the people in this working-class area of London struggle, scheme and try to better themselves, but everything seems destined to fail. Even the crooks fall easy prey to the coppers. The politics of the film, although seemingly liberal in its earnest portrait of working-class life, are basically conservative; the subtext suggests that perhaps it is best to accept your fate and not expect to make real changes to your life.

Googie Withers was one of the few actresses, employed in British movies of this era, who could embody sensuality and she is excellent in the role of the housewife who nearly gives everything up for a wild, destructive passion for the wrong man. Her real-life husband John McCallum was never better than in his role as the man on the run. There are also memorable performances from Sydney Tafler, Edward Chapman and Susan Shaw. Robert Hamer, who was something of a stylist in film, would go on to make the Ealing comedy classic *Kind Hearts and Coronets*. Douglas Slocombe's photography is marvellous and although most of the footage is studio-bound, the atmosphere and look of London's East End are represented with admirable authenticity. *It Always Rains on Sundays* looks forward to the British New Wave of the 1960s when directors such as Karel Reisz, Tony Richardson and John Schlesinger would aim to represent working-class life with a new veracity.

Hamlet (1948)

Crew: directed by Laurence Olivier; produced by Laurence Olivier; screenplay by Alan Dent, based on the play by William Shakespeare; cinematography by Desmond Dickinson; edited by Helga Cranston; music by William Walton; production design by Roger Furse; art direction by Carmen Dillon; costumes by Elizabeth Hennings. B&W. 155 mins.

Cast: Laurence Olivier (Hamlet); Eileen Herlie (Gerturde); Basil Sidney (Claudius); Jean Simmons (Ophelia); Felix Aylmer (Polonius); Norman Wooland (Horatio); Stanley Holloway (Gravedigger).

Olivier, in the second Shakespearian movie he directed, reduced the tragedy of Hamlet to a story about a man who could not make up his mind. While rather simplistic, the movie survives this approach, although the text and the characters had to necessarily be cut to fit into a movie of about two-and-a half-hours. The characters of Rosencrantz and Guildenstern are missing, for example, which offended the purists as did the fact that Olivier, about 40 when he made the film, was demonstrably too old for Hamlet, especially as his screen mother was played by Eileen Herlie who was a few years younger than him in reality.

Opinions divide sharply about Olivier's performance and the movie itself. For many people, the long dolly shots of Elsinore and the use of deep-focus photography in general detract from the action and the poetry of Shakespeare's dramatic verse. However, a doom-laden atmosphere is successfully created and the film is seldom static, which is the danger when adapting Shakespeare to the screen. Clearly, Olivier was determined to make a film, not a record of a stage production. Olivier has also been criticised for being mannered and self-indulgent, yet he was one of the few British classical actors with a real physical presence both on stage and on film. He manages to convince as the tortured Hamlet and never speaks the verse with less than total authority and instinctive understanding.

The tricky ghost scenes are effectively staged, the fencing climax between Hamlet and Laertes is terrific, and Olivier brings a perfect sense of comic timing to the scenes where Hamlet is acting 'crazy'. Norman Wooland is perfectly cast as Hamlet's best friend and look out for a cameo appearance by Peter Cushing as the preening Osric. One of the master-strokes Olivier employed in his Shakespearian adaptations was to employ William Walton to write the musical scores. Walton's score for Hamlet perfectly underlines the brooding melancholy of the film. The black-and-white photography by Desmond Dickinson reinforces the tragic nature of the action. Olivier's *Hamlet* is not the perfect Shakespearian screen adaptation of the play, but only the 1964 Russian film comes anywhere near its quality.

Oliver Twist (1948)

Crew: directed by David Lean; produced by Anthony Havelock-Allen and Ronald Neame; screenplay by David Lean and Stanley Haynes based on the novel by Charles Dickens; cinematography by Guy Green; edited by Jack

Harris; music by Arnold Bax; costumes by Margaret Furse; production design by John Bryan. B&W. 105 mins.

Cast: Robert Newton (Bill Sykes); Alec Guinness (Fagin); Kay Walsh (Nancy); Francis L Sullivan (Mr Bumble); Henry Stephenson (Mr Brownlow); Mary Clare (Mrs Corney); John Howard Davies (Oliver Twist); Josephine Stuart (Oliver's mother); Anthony Newley (The Artful Dodger).

Oliver Twist is an example of the talents of British film technicians employed almost to their fullest extent. John Bryan's production design for the teeming London streets, Fagin's lair and the waterside haunts of Bill Sykes are particularly memorable, as is Guy Green's cinematography. The editing of Jack Harris and Margaret Furse's costume design are equally fine and the whole movie looks splendid and as authentically Victorian as a film representation can be. British companies are very good at producing this kind of period drama, perhaps too good at times, so that the temptation is to produce more and more heritage cinema.

David Lean, with his co-writer Stanley Haynes, skilfully managed to reduce Dickens' novel to fit the confines of a standard-length feature and Lean's ability to tell a story in pictures is evident in various vivid scenes, such as the opening sequence where Oliver's pregnant mother arrives at the workhouse door or the hunt for Bill Sykes. Alec Guinness's portrayal of Fagin has been called anti-semitic and an actor playing the role nowadays would certainly have second thoughts about donning such stereotypical make-up and acting 'Jewish'. However, Guinness always had a tendency towards racial stereotyping in his roles, witness his lamentable Professor Godbole in Lean's *A Passage to India* and his Arab prince in *Lawrence of Arabia*. Robert

Newton hams it up as usual as the villainous Sykes, whilst Kay Walsh, at that time married to David Lean, makes a sympathetic Nancy.

Movies such as *Oliver Twist* are not examples of British filmmaking at its most adventurous. On the contrary, films like these reflect the industry's reliance on literary sources. However, in the hands of people who know what they are doing in terms of tone, style and period, *Oliver Twist* remains a very enjoyable film adaptation of Dickens.

The Fallen Idol (1948)

Crew: directed by Carol Reed; produced by David Selznick and Carol Reed; screenplay by Graham Greene, Lesley Storm and William Templeton, based on the short story 'The Basement Room' by Graham Greene; cinematography by Georges Perinal; edited by Oswald Halenrichter; music by William Alwyn; production design by Vincent Korda, James Sawyer and John Hawkesworth. B&W. 94 mins.

Cast: Ralph Richardson (Baines); Michele Morgan (Julie); Bobby Henry (Felipe); Sonia Dresdel (Mrs Baines); Denis O'Dea (Inspector Crowe); Walter Fitzgerald (Dr Fenton); Karen Stepanek (First Secretary); Jack Hawkins (Detective-sergeant); Dora Bryan (woman in police station).

Novelist Graham Greene found his perfect collaborator in director Carol Reed. Adapting the screenplay from his own short story, Greene explores the conflicting loyalties and guilts of a young boy involved in the intrigues and enmities of the adult world. Richardson plays a butler in a foreign embassy in London who is married to a shrewish, dislikeable wife (excellently played by Sonia Dresdel), and who is having an affair with the embassy temp, played by beautiful French actress Michele Morgan. Richardson may be a trifle too impeccably middle-class as the butler and Morgan seems an unlikely lover for such a man, but despite these quibbles, both give laudable performances. The revelation, however, is in the performance of Bobby Henrey as the boy. He thinks he has witnessed the murder of the wife by Baines and in his attempts to protect his surrogate father, he only succeeds in alerting the suspicions of the investigating police into the possibility that Mrs Baines has indeed been murdered. Reed manages to elicit from Henrey a touching representation of a child trying in vain to make sense of the adult world and in doing so, landing his hero, the butler, in hot water.

The Fallen Idol received a British Best Film award and Reed was voted Best Director by the New York Film Critics. The film is beautifully constructed, subtle and conveys an adult world through the eyes of a child most convincingly. The embassy set is a terrific piece of cinematic design by Vincent Korda and Reed also uses exterior scenes to great effect, including a scene at London Zoo. Noteworthy supporting players include Jack Hawkins as a policeman and Dora Bryan as a prostitute. *The Fallen Idol* was intelligent fare for the mass audience of the time and although it garnered critical praise, it was only modestly successful at the box-office. However, it remains one of the very best British films ever made.

Whisky Galore (1948)

Crew: directed by Alexander Mackendrick; produced by Monja Danischewky; screenplay by Compton Mackenzie and Angus Macphail from the novel by Compton Mackenzie; cinematography by Gerald Gibbs; music by Ernest Irving. B&W. 82 mins.

Cast: Basil Radford (Captain Waggett); Joan Greenwood (Peggy Macroon); Jean Cadell (Mrs Campbell); Gordon Jackson (George Campbell); James Robertson Justice (Dr Maclaren); Wylie Watson (Joseph Macroon); Duncan Macrae (Angus McCormac); Catherine Lacey (Mrs Waggett); Bruce Seton (Sergeant Odd).

During World War II, a ship carrying cargo of good Scotch whisky runs aground off the shore of a Hebridean island. The islanders, suffering from a whisky drought because of wartime privations, seize the opportunity to raid the ship and make off with the whisky, despite the efforts of the local busybody in the shape of an English army type who sees it as his duty to prevent such illegal smuggling. That is the simple plot structure of *Whisky Galore*, the screenplay of which was adapted by Compton Mackenzie, author of the original novel on which the film is based.

The movie continually flirts with (and topples over into) national stereotyping, with the Scots portrayed as living for their next dram, but the theme is handled with such charm by the excellent cast and director, Alexander Mackendrick, that these reservations are largely swept aside. Ealing Comedy invariably dealt in such stereotypes and, instead of the plucky Cockneys of *Passport to Pimlico* or the resourceful English villagers of *The Titfield Thunderbolt*, here we have crafty Hebrideans who can outsmart the forces of law and order to gain their due share of 'the water of heaven'. Mackendrick would go on to direct two of Ealing's biggest comedy successes, *The Man in the White Suit* and *The Ladykillers*, as well as another Scottish comedy, *The Maggie*. Mackendrick also directed one of the best Hollywood movies of the 1950s, *Sweet Smell of Success*.

Great Scottish character actors such as Duncan Macrae, Wylie Watson, Jean Cadell and James Robertson Justice lend genuine authenticity to the enterprise, whilst Basil Radford and Catherine Lacey are excellent as the bemused English. Joan Greenwood makes a husky-voiced appearance and there is an early role for Gordon Jackson.

The film is quite short at 82 minutes, but it moves with such pace and represents such a rich picture of the Hebridean community that its brevity does not detract from the overall effectiveness. Indeed, because it moves along and makes its points with such a sure comic touch, it is in little danger of outstaying its welcome.

The Red Shoes (1948)

Crew: directed by Michael Powell and Emeric Pressburger; produced by Michael Powell and Emeric Pressburger; screenplay by Emeric Pressburger, Michael Powell and Keith Winter; cinematography by Jack Cardiff; edited by Reginald Mills; music by Brian Easdale; art direction by Hein Heckroth and Arthur Lawson; choreography by Robert Helpmann; costumes by Hein Heckroth. Colour. 133 mins.

Cast: Anton Walbrook (Lermontov); Moira Shearer (Victoria Page); Marius Goring (Julian Craster); Leonide Massine (Grischa Ljubov); Robert Helpmann (Ivan Boleslawsky); Esmond Knight (Livy); Ludmilla Tcherina (Irina Boronskaja); Jean Short (Terry).

A pretentious, high camp melodrama about the demands of the artistic life or a truly cinematic extravaganza of colour, dance, music, production design and acting? This movie still divides opinion though many see it as one of the greatest British movies of all time. It cannot be denied that the film consistently flirts with outrageous melodrama and then finally at the end topples into it with the suicide of the ballerina played by Moira Shearer jumping, or rather floating, to her death in Monte Carlo. This is followed by the highly-mannered curtain speech by the impresario played by Anton Walbrook, who has to announce to the audience that his star ballerina will not be able to appear. Nevertheless, despite the overall campness and its air of preciousness, the film is terrific to look at and at the core of it is a wonderful twenty-minute ballet sequence, which gives the movie its title.

Moira Shearer, at that time a ballerina with the Sadler's Wells Ballet, plays Victoria, a young dancer given her chance in the ballet company run by the imperious and driven Lermontov (Walbrook). She has a triumph in a ballet especially created for her, 'The Red Shoes', based on Hans Christian Anderson's tale of a pair of ballet shoes that allows a young girl to dance magically but which won't allow her to stop dancing. The ballerina marries a young composer (Marius Goring) much against the wishes of Lermontov, who banishes her and prevents her from dancing for other companies. He relents to allow her to dance the role once more in Monaco, which means that she will miss the premiere of one of her husband's symphonies. Page/Shearer is so torn between her love of the dance and its impossible demands and her love for her husband that she takes that swan-like dive into the depths of Monaco.

The theme of the woman torn between her artistic life

and her private life seems rather dated now: no such tensions appear to be a problem in her husband's life, although he is equally dedicated to his profession. Powell and Pressburger seem to be making a point about the dangers of the obsessive artistic life and the destruction that such single-minded devotion can wreak on an individual's private life, but it is somewhat on the overheated side. The core ballet represents the theme in dance and here the movie really comes to its peak of artistic achievement. Helpmann's choreography is expertly adapted to the medium of film, Jack Cardiff's colour photography is truly memorable, the design is terrific and Shearer's dancing sublime.

In the great Michael Powell movies, style transcends most weaknesses of theme, plot, acting and tone, and that remains true of *The Red Shoes*. It is a movie with serious flaws, but it cannot be discounted because of the confidence with which it takes the visual possibilities of cinema and exploits them with imagination and real flair.

Saraband For Dead Lovers (1948)

Crew: directed by Basil Dearden and Michael Relph; produced by Michael Relph; screenplay by John Dighton and Alexander Mackendrick, from the novel by Helen Simpson; cinematography by Douglas Slocombe; music by Alan Rawsthorne; edited by Jim Morahan, William Kellner and Michael Relph. Technicolour. 96 mins.

Cast: Stewart Granger (Philip Konigsmark), Joan Greenwood (Sophia Dorothea), Francoise Rosay (Electress Sophia), Flora Robson (Countess Clara Platen); Peter Bull (Prince George Louis); Anthony Quayle (Durer); Michael Gough (Prince Charles).

It was unusual for Ealing Studios to splash out on an expensive historical drama and the box-office failure of *Saraband* led to Michael Balcon, the head of production at the studio, to put an end to such costly films. The public turned its back on this offering; the reviews tipped them off that this historical drama was not one of the bodice-ripping melodramas such *The Wicked Lady* and *The Man in Grey* that Gainsborough Studios had made so much money with. It may be that *Saraband* could have done with some of the melodrama that was poured into those escapist yarns: a major criticism of the film is that it is too bloodless and there is no sense of real tragedy about the central love affair between Sophie Dorothea, wife of the Elector of Hanover who later became George I of England, and Count Konigsmark, a Swedish adventurer, killed at the end of the film so that the Hanovarian ambitions are not thwarted by an illicit love affair.

The lovers, Stewart Granger and Joan Greenwood, never spark off one another, hardly surprising given that Granger's appeal was never of the subtle variety whilst Greenwood's screen persona was much more quirky and ambivalent. What is memorable about the movie is the production design, the costumes and the cinematography of Douglas Slocombe. The film looks luscious whilst at the same time Slocombe manages to convey the murky prison that the Hanovarian court has become for the lovers. The style of the film becomes more important than the action, the dialogue or the rather stilted acting; the real meaning is communicated through the visual qualities. The gloominess of the theme and the fates of the leading characters may have put contemporary audiences off; this was, after all, in the post-war years when cinemagoers were looking for films to take their minds off austerity and the beginnings of the Cold War. The makers of *Saraband for Dead Lovers* at least deserve credit for making the potentially uncommercial movie it turned out to be.

Kind Hearts and Coronets (1949)

Crew: directed by Robert Hamer; produced by Michael Balcon; screenplay by Robert Hamer and John Dighton based on the novel 'Israel Rank' by Roy Horniman; cinematography by Douglas Slocombe; edited by Peter Tanner; music by Mozart from 'Don Giovanni'; art direction by William Kellner. B&W. 105 mins.

Cast: Dennis Price (Louis Mazzini); Valerie Hobson (Edith D'Ascoyne); Joan Greenwood (Sibella); Alec Guinness (The Duke/The Banker/The Parson/The General/The Admiral/ Young Ascoyne/D'Ascoyne/Lady Agatha); Audrey Fides (Mama); Miles Malleson (The Hangman); Clive Morton (Prison Governor); John Penrose (Lionel); Cecil Ramage (Crown Counsel); Hugh Griffith (Lord High Steward).

This is Ealing comedy near its best. Robert Hamer, along with Alexander Mackendrick, were the most talented directors to work for the studio. Hamer co-wrote the script with John Dighton and it achieves an eloquence and wit rare in British movies.

The storyline is quite simple: Dennis Price plays an impoverished distant branch of an aristocratic family who is determined to inherit the dukedom which he feels is due to him because of the manner in which the family had treated his mother. He insinuates his way into the family life in a way that gives him access to the individuals who stand in his way and he systematically proceeds to bump off six of them whilst two others die in accidents. He inherits the dukedom, but after being cleared for a murder he did not actually commit, he leaves behind in the prison a journal that is in fact a confession that will take him to the gallows. This film was made in 1949 and so murder and crime in general had to be seen not to pay, hence this tacked-on ending which satisfied the moralists, but it is clear where the sympathies of the movie lie and it is not with the victims of the aspiring lower-class assassin.

This is black comedy, but the tone is largely light and satirical. The aristocrats are portrayed as either nasty and selfish or dotty and useless. Does *Kind Hearts and Coronets* voice some kind of social criticism of Britain in the 1940s? The film is actually set at the turn of the century, but it can be read as a representation of a contemporary aristocratic class in its death throes. The Dennis Price character is representative of the thrusting middle-class eager to take over from the decadent and useless aristos. The film was made four years after the Labour Government under Clement Attlee had been elected, with a massive landslide in its favour. The country had voted for the ending of old aristocratic Tory rule; *Kind Hearts and Coronets* could be seen as embodying some of this new radicalism.

Most of the praise for the actors has been directed towards Alec Guinness for his multiple roles as the members of the D'Ascoyne family, but this has been overdone. His performance owes more to the make-up department than anything else and his portrayals rarely rise above the level of 'clever turns'. Dennis Price, however, is suitably cold and waspish as the anti-hero, whilst Joan Greenwood and Valerie Hobson are excellent as the women in his life. The production values are of the highest and once again the cinematography of Douglas Slocombe is top-notch.

Kind Hearts and Coronets is one of the best British comedies of all time.

The Third Man (1949)

Crew: directed by Carol Reed; produced by David Selznick; screenplay by Graham Greene; cinematography by Robert Krasker; music by Anton Karas; edited by Oswald Hafenrichter; production design by Vincent Korda, Joseph Bata and John Hawkesworth. B&W. 104 mins.

Cast: Joseph Cotten (Holly Martins); Orson Welles (Harry Lime); Alida Valli (Anna Schmidt); Trevor Howard (Major Calloway); Bernard Lee (Sergeant Paine); Ernst Deutsch (Baron Kurtz); Erich Ponto (Dr Winkel); Siegfried Breuer (Popescu).

This movie marks the high point for the artistic collaboration between director Carol Reed and novelist and screenwriter Graham Greene. Set in immediate post-World War II Vienna, the movie establishes the ruined grandeur of the city as a character in its own right. Krasker's brilliant lighting and Reed's imaginative directing make full use of the sinister qualities of dark, empty, cobbled streets, decayed buildings and, in the penultimate sequence, of the Vienna sewers.

It is a tale of friendship, love, betrayal and the attractiveness of evil, an apt theme for the post-Hitler era. Cotten plays the weak, vacillating American friend of Harry Lime, a cynical black marketeer out to profit from post-war shortages in a city divided among the four major powers of the time. Orson Welles is the charismatic bad guy, loved by Alida Valli, whom Cotten falls for and who spurns him at the end of the movie because he has betrayed Lime/Welles to the authorities. Graham Greene once famously said that if ever it came to a choice between betraying a close friend and betraying his country, he hoped he would have the courage to betray his country. Such provocative statements helped build the mystique surrounding Greene with his wartime spying activities in Africa for MI5 and his association with the Cambridge spies, Burgess, Maclean and Anthony Blunt. It is easy to see how the central theme of *The Third Man*, the tug of loyalties between the American's friendship for bad guy Lime and his duty to help the authorities to arrest a criminal who sold doctored penicillin on the Viennese black market, reflected aspects of Greene's own life and friendships.

It could not have been easy for Reed to direct Orson Welles, who, being the egotist he was, wrote many of his own memorable lines including this speech: 'In Italy for thirty years under the Borgias, they had warfare, terror, murder and bloodshed, but they produced Michaelangelo, Leonardo da Vinci and the Renaissance. In Switzerland they had brotherly love; they had five hundred years of democracy and peace – and what did that produce? The cuckoo clock.' Another master-stroke was using Anton Karas' zither music as the score. The music underscores the closing sequence in the cemetery when Cotten, having witnessed the burial of the friend he has betrayed, waits at the end of a long path for the woman he has fallen in love with and who has loved Lime: she passes him without a word or a glance his way. It is a masterful reassertion of the main theme of the movie.

The film is popular entertainment for the mass market that manages to create a lasting resonance about the dangers of charismatic figures and the loyalty they inspire.

The Third Man is a strong candidate for the title of the best British movie ever made.

Other Notable British Films of this Period

49th Parallel (1941)
In Which We Serve (1942)
Fires Were Started (documentary) (1943)
The Man in Grey (1943)
A Canterbury Tale (1944)
Waterloo Road (1944)
This Happy Breed (1944)
I Know Where I'm Going (1945)
Dead of Night (1945)
The Wicked Lady (1945)
Blithe Spirit (1945)
Green for Danger (1946)
Mine Own Executioner (1947)
Scott of the Antarctic (1948)
Passport to Pimlico (1949)
The Small Back Room (1948)
The Queen of Spades (1949)

Fighting for the Mass Audience: 1950–59

In the 1950s, television became established as the major form of mass entertainment, in Britain, in the States and all over Europe. A television set in almost every home in the land inevitably led to a sharp decrease in the number of cinema tickets sold. As an example, in the USA the number of weekly tickets sold halved between 1946 and 1956 from 90 million to 45 million. This major decrease in box-office revenues meant that the major studios had to cut their cloth accordingly. Long-term contracts for stars, directors and technical staff became a thing of the past as the number of feature films produced dramatically decreased. Hollywood saw the beginning of the break-up of the studio system.

The Rank Organisation and Associated British Pictures, the two main British production companies, also felt the pinch and gradually both organisations withdrew from direct film financing and rid themselves of permanent rosters of actors and other personnel. Whereas Hollywood would pin its faith in the 1950s on new technologies, such as the introduction of Cinemascope and Vistavision, British producers largely opted for 'broad appeal' in their attempts to shore up ticket sales. The result was the 'Doctor in the House' series, the start of the 'Carry On' romps and numerous other slapstick comedies starring the likes of Ronald Shiner, Norman Wisdom and Brian Rix. Ealing comedy continued to thrive, with one-off super hits such as *Genevieve*. With the war still fresh in the nation's memory, war movies were continually churned out, most of which were fairly pedestrian, with a few outstanding exceptions.

James Mason and Stewart Granger had departed for Hollywood, the careers of the female stars of the Gainsborough melodramas were in decline, and a new generation of British stars were taking their place. Dirk Bogarde became the rather unlikely number-one British heartthrob, Jack Hawkins the British gentleman star par excellence, Richard Attenborough and John Mills the stalwarts of the British screen, whilst Peter Finch, Stanley Baker and Richard Todd also experienced popularity. Diana Dors, Sylvia Sims and Virginia McKenna were among the new generation of British female stars, with Audrey Hepburn and Jean Simmons having been taken up by Hollywood early on in their careers.

The 1950s was also the decade of the British 'B' movie. Due to financial restrictions imposed by the British government, Hollywood had money tied up in the country and bankrolled 'B' movies, which often starred minor American stars such as Alex Nicol, Dane Clark and Arlene Dahl. These films would make up the first half of a double bill, a ploy to give cinemagoers value for money in the continuing attempt to wean audiences away from their television sets. An alternative to the 'B' movie was often short crime features such as the Edgar Lustgarten series, guaranteed to keep the audiences in fits of laughter at the creaky production values and second-rate plots and acting.

The days of an Odeon and an ABC cinema on every high street in the land were numbered. By the end of the decade, cinemas were closing in great numbers to be replaced by Bingo halls. The second-run chains were badly hit and the old fleapits lost their attraction. The heyday of the cinema as a truly unrivalled mass entertainment was over.

The Man in the White Suit (1951)

Crew: directed by Alexander Mackendrick; produced by Michael Balcon; screenplay by Roger MacDougall, John Dighton and Alexander Mackendrick based on the play by Roger MacDougall; cinematography by Douglas Slocombe; edited by Bernard Gribble; music by Benjamin Frankel; art direction by Jim Morahan. B&W. 81 mins.

Cast: Alec Guinness (Sidney Stratton); Joan Greenwood (Daphne Birnley); Cecil Parker (Alan Birnley); Michael Gough (Michael Corland); Ernest Thesiger (Sir John Kierlaw); Howard Marion-Crawford (Cranford); Duncan Lamont (Harry); Henry Mollison (Hoskins); Vida Hope (Betha); Patric Doonan (Frank).

The Man in the White Suit was Alexander Mackendrick's second major success for Ealing. It tells the tale of an inventor (Guinness) who discovers a method of producing a cloth that will never wear out and repels dirt instantly, hence the white suit of the title. At first, this discovery is greeted with great enthusiasm by his employers and the work force until it sinks in that it has serious implications for production and work prospects. Clothes that never wear out or never need cleaning would mean a drastic fall in demand, thereby threatening manufacturers' profits and the jobs of the workers. Opposition thus mounts and the process is destroyed. A gentle satire of capitalism and unionism, made in the Ealing tradition, it seems to take a broadly consensual line regarding the politics of the basic situation.

Mackendrick had a hand in writing the script and his overall input dominates. He adds a much-needed asperity to Ealing comedies, which otherwise tended towards cosiness and whimsy. He is well-served by his cast. Alec Guinness garnered most of the critical praise, but Joan Greenwood, Cecil Parker, Ernest Thesiger and Vida Hope, among others, provide sterling support. The film has pace and is quite short, much like Mackendrick's earlier success *Whisky Galore*. Once again, authority and bureaucracy are challenged and although the inventor seems to be defeated at the end of the movie, he clearly has intentions of producing another discovery that will shake up the industry. As a social document of its times, *The Man in the White Suit* represents a Britain unwilling to face up to innovation and mired in old-fashioned capitalist-worker conflict.

Scrooge (1951)

Crew: directed by Brian Desmond-Hurst; produced by Brian Desmond-Hurst; cinematography by C Pennington-Richards; screenplay by Noel Langley based on the novel 'The Christmas Carol' by Charles Dickens; music by Richard Addinsell. B&W. 86 mins.

Cast: Alistair Sim (Scrooge); Mervyn Johns (Bob Crachit); Kathleen Harris (Mrs Dilber); Jack Warner (Mr Jorkin); Michael Hordern (Jacob Marley/Marley's Ghost); Hermione Baddely (Mrs Cratchit); George Cole (Young Scrooge); Rona Anderson (Alice).

Dickens' *Christmas Carol* has been filmed several times, but this is by far the most successful version, partly because in Alistair Sim, there was a perfect match of actor and character. Sim brings his own idiosyncratic brand of Scottish gloominess to the role of the miserly Scrooge. His lugubrious face, his air of expecting nothing from life or people, his miserable aspect, are integral to the part and he milks it for all its worth. The danger with this Dickensian parable is its lapse into ghastly sentimentality over the poor Cratchits and Tiny Tim in particular. The darker elements of the story – Scrooge's sheer nastiness as a miserly employer, the scenes of his youth when he is hurt by a rejection in love – dominate the film.

In addition to the outstanding Sim, there is a plethora of distinguished supporting actors: Mervyn Johns as Cratchit, the inimitable Kathleen Harris as Mrs Cratchit, Michael Hordern as the ghost of Christmas Past and George Cole, a protégé of Sim's, as the young Scrooge. Victorian London is convincingly recreated in the studio and Pennington-Richard's cinematography is outstanding. Once again, this is a British film that has literature as its source, but provides further evidence of the skill and understanding with which British filmmakers can translate literature into film.

The Lavender Hill Mob (1951)

Crew: directed by Charles Crichton; produced by Michael Balcon; screenplay by T E B Clarke; cinematography by Douglas Slocombe; edited by Seth Holt; music by Georges Auric; art direction by William Kellner. B&W. 82 mins.

Cast: Alec Guinness (Henry Holland); Stanley Holloway (Pendlebury); Sidney James (Lackery); Alfie Bass (Shorty); Marjorie Fielding (Mrs Chalk); John Gregson (Farrow); Edie Martin (Miss Evesham); Clive Morton (Station Sergeant); Ronald Adam (Turner); Sydney Tafler (Clayton).

Comic crooks are a staple element of Ealing in particular and British film comedy in general, and *The Lavender Hill Mob* and *The Ladykillers* are the cream of this sub-genre. The plot of *The Lavender Hill Mob* revolves round the unlikely heist of gold bullion by Guinness, a mild-mannered employee of the bullion company, Holloway, who is a manufacturer of paper weights, and two professional crooks, Sid James in his pre-'Carry On' days and Alfie Bass, a British film veteran. The story is told in flashback by the Guinness character now in Rio, although he has been arrested by a Scotland Yard detective: crime could never be seen to pay in those far-off days so the crooks, comic or not, have to be apprehended.

This is Ealing comedy at near its cosiest, and the film lacks the edge that Alexander Mackendrick brought to the studio's output. To enjoy the movie, you have to suspend your disbelief that such a couple of amiable duffers could mastermind this kind of heist and get away with it, or that there ever existed such lovable Clapham criminals of the kind played by James and Bass. Characteristically pacy and brief, the story is told well within 90 minutes, with not a frame wasted.

Genevieve (1953)

Crew: directed by Henry Cornelius; produced by Henry Cornelius; screenplay by William Rose; cinematography by Christopher Challis; edited by Clive Donner; music by Larry Adler. Colour. 86 mins.

Cast: John Gregson (Alan McKim); Dinah Sheridan (Wendy McKim); Kenneth More (Ambrose Claverhouse); Kay Kendall (Rosalind Peters); Geoffrey Keen (1st Speed

Cop); Harold Siddons (2nd Speed Cop); Reginald
Beckwith (J C Callahan); Anthony Wontner (Elderly
Gentleman); Joyce Grenfell (Hotel Proprietress).

This was one of the most successful British movies of the
1950s. It represents an England of old-world charm, an
England that is comfortably well-off and middle-class, and
obsessed with classic cars. Centred round an annual British
ritual, the London to Brighton Antique Car Rally, the main
characters are four personable people who live rather glamorous lives and reside in London mews houses. Their main
concerns are marital flirtations and which of the two
couples will win an unofficial race. It all adds up to an
escapist comedy for 1950s cinemagoers still struggling with
post-war deprivations.

The screenplay is by an American writer, William Rose,
who clearly had a somewhat fustian view of British society,
seeing in it a grace and good manners that contemporary
America lacked. There is a telling moment at the end of the
movie when the John Gregson character, at the climax of
the race, is too polite to drive away from an old gentleman
who has stopped beside his stationary 1904 roadster to have
an admiring chat. However, despite the hero seeming to
have forfeited his chances of winning, he triumphs in the
end when the cad's car is caught up in tram rails and drives
in the wrong direction. The implication seems to be that
good manners maketh the man and class will win out in the
end.

What many people remember about the film is Larry
Adler's harmonica score, a masterstroke that underscores
the quaintness of the entire concept. It certainly made a star
of Kenneth More, who would go on to play his bluff, golf
club, saloon bar bore in many a British comedy. It was also

a particular success for Kay Kendall, who, like her co-star John Gregson, died prematurely. The Technicolor cinematography by Christopher Challis is terrific and presents a picture of south-east England before the M25 and the motorways that encroached into the English countryside. As usual in British film comedy, the supporting character actors provide good value and there is a particularly effective cameo performance by Joyce Grenfell as the proprietor of an eccentric Brighton hotel. British filmmakers were not averse to serving up this image of an eccentric, out-of-date country for external consumption, and American cinemagoers, in turn, were perhaps comforted by this representation of an England that seemed to live in the past and posed no real challenge to their emerging dominance.

The Maggie (1954)

Crew: directed by Alexander Mackendrick; produced by Michael Truman; screenplay by William Rose; cinematography by Gordon Dines; music by John Addison. B&W. 93 mins.

Cast: Paul Douglas (Calvin B. Marshall); Alex Mackenzie (Skipper Mactaggart); James Copeland (The First Mate); Abe Barker (The Engineer); Tommy Kearins (The Wee Boy).

William Rose, screenwriter of *Genevieve*, once again penned a representation of Britain stuck in its old ways, resistant to modern tempos and demands, in *The Maggie*. This time the setting is Scotland. A brash American businessman has an urgent need to ship equipment to a remote Scottish island. A wily Scottish skipper tricks him into giving him the job and the bulk of the movie concerns the crew's attempts to hoodwink their employer and cover up the fact that their boat, the Maggie of the title, is totally unseaworthy and inadequate for its task. All's well that ends well and the American learns some humility and humanity by the end of the movie, allowing grudging respect to the crafty highlanders.

Paul Douglas is the only star of the movie. The rest of the cast are mainly Scottish character actors, with Alex Mackenzie outstanding as the skipper of the Maggie. Ealing comedies delighted in old things and people: ancient castles and customs, old trains and, in this case, old boats. All are affectionately satirized here, but at the heart of Ealing comedy is a Britain that had already largely vanished. There is no doubt where the sympathies of *The Maggie* lie and it is not with the rich businessman, well played by the reliable and underrated Douglas. Just as in *Genevieve*, William Rose serves up a picture of Britain that is comforting and nostalgic, in which the imperatives of work and making a buck are secondary to preserving a way of life that was under threat. Bill Forsyth's 1978 movie *Local Hero*, in which Burt Lancaster plays the high-powered American businessman who is entranced by the charm of the Scottish islands and gives up his driven life, was clearly influenced by *The Maggie*.

Outcast of the Islands (1951)

Crew: directed by Carol Reed; produced by Carol Reed; screenplay by William Fairchild from the novel by Joseph Conrad; cinematography by John Wilcox; music by Brian Easdale. B&W. 102 mins.

Cast: Trevor Howard (Willems); Ralph Richardson (Captain Lingard); Kerima (Aissa); Robert Morley

(Almayer); Wendy Hiller (Mrs Almayer); George Coulouris (Babalatch); Frederick Valk (Hudig).

Adapted by William Fairchild from Joseph Conrad's novel, this is one of the most underrated of Carol Reed's directorial efforts. It also has a great central performance by one of the very best of British film actors, Trevor Howard. Set in the Far East, in the days when sailing ships were still in operation, it tells of the gradual degradation of the amoral and opportunistic Willems (played by Howard). Captain Lingard (Ralph Richardson) gives him a golden opportunity to put his unsavoury past behind him by imparting the secret of invaluable trading routes and contacts. Willems betrays his benefactor and he is expelled from the European community once more. His degradation is linked to his sexual obsession with the beautiful daughter of an indigenous chieftain. The end of the film sees the avenging Lingard deciding not to shoot Willems, but to leave him isolated from his own people, despised by his woman and her community, who are unable to understand why he does not kill his former benefactor.

Joseph Conrad's race politics were rarely politically correct and this is reflected in the film. Viewed from a contemporary perspective, the emphasis on the antihero's sexual 'disgrace' as the symbol of his degradation is less than palatable, but there is a convincing sense of inevitable doom about his slide towards a tragic fate. The last scene, shot amidst monsoon rains, when his benefactor sails away from the isolated island where Willems is holed up with his paramour, is chilling in its finality.

Howard was a very physical actor, never reluctant to look less than glamorous on screen, and he communicates exactly the insecure cockiness of the amoral Willems.

71

Richardson is authoritative as his mentor and Wendy Hiller is extremely effective as the wife of an oafish ex-pat, played by the eye-popping Robert Morley.

Heart of the Matter (1953)

Crew: directed by George More O'Ferrall; screenplay by Ian Dalrymple and Lesley Storm based on the novel by Graham Greene; cinematography by Jack Hillyard; music by Brian Easdale. B&W. 105 mins.

Crew: Trevor Howard (Scobie); Maria Schell (Helen Rolt); Elizabeth Allan (Louise Scobie); Denholm Elliott (Wilson); Peter Finch (Father Rank); Gerard Oury (Yusef); George Coulouris (Portuguese captain); Michael Hordern (Polce Commissioner).

Trevor Howard's performance as a guilt-ridden commissioner of police in Sierra Leone in 1942 is reason enough for this movie to be reassessed. No British actor could represent despair and a compromised integrity better than Howard. Perhaps because in his own life he battled with alcoholism for much of the time, he was able to play a man on the edge of self-destruction so convincingly. Howard's ravaged face stood him in good stead, and he played thinking men with ease, a rare quality among British movie stars of this period.

Scobie is basically a good man who tries to do his best in his life and job. A Catholic, he is consumed with guilt about the unhappiness of his neurotic wife (played all too convincingly by Elizabeth Allan) and this guilt is only increased when he has an illicit affair with a young widow whose ship has been sunk by the Germans. He is then caught between his duty towards his wife and his love for the needy young woman. To raise money to send his wife to South Africa for a holiday, he becomes involved with a local criminal with inevitable results. In the novel, Scobie commits suicide. Although Scobie dies at the end of the film, the film fudges this issue.

Heart of the Matter was made on a tight budget and the production values are not of the highest, but Jack Hillyard's cinematography is nevertheless top-notch. Denholm Elliott plays a young man in love with Scobie's wife, a precursor to the seedy roles that he would later make his forte. Although not a great film, *Heart of the Matter* is a very interesting, if compromised, attempt to adapt a Greene novel; and at its core is a terrific performance by Trevor Howard.

The Dam Busters (1954)

Crew: directed by Michael Anderson; produced by Robert Clark; screenplay by RC Sheriff from the books by Guy Gibson and Paul Brickhill; cinematography by Erwin Hillier; music by Leighton Lucas and Eric Coates. B&W. 125 mins.

Cast: Michael Redgrave (Barnes Wallis); Richard Todd (Guy Gibson); Basil Sydney (Sir Arthur Harris); Derek Farr (Group-Captain Whitworth); Patrick Barr (Captain Joseph Summer); Ursula Jeans (Mrs Wallis).

This is one of the quintessential British war movies. It tells the story of the successful 1943 attack on the Ruhr dams using bouncing bombs invented by Barnes Wallis. How effective and necessary this mission was has been the subject of dispute in recent years, but there is no doubt about the effectiveness of the film's myth-making.

Although Michael Anderson's direction has been praised, it is RC Sheriff's screenplay, Michael Redgrave's acting, Erwin Hillier's black-and-white cinematography and Eric Coates' stirring *Dam Busters March* that are its most memorable features. Sheriff was the author of the First World War classic *Journey's End* and he brought a rare quality to the scripts of British war movies that tended to dwell in the main on public school repartee and stiff-upper-lip clichés. The highly-skilled and underrated Redgrave underplays as the obsessive Barnes Wallis. Hillier's nighttime photography adds immensely to the film's impact and although we know we are watching models, the raid itself is convincing. The raid on the dams was 'borrowed' by George Lucas for the attack on the Death Star sequence in the first of the *Star Wars* movies. The floods that engulf the surrounding territory after the raid were actual floods filmed in Germany at the time of the making of the movie. It is impossible to think of *The Dam Busters* now without Eric Coates' pastiche score.

Richard Todd is rather stiff as hero Guy Gibson, but then his character functions as a symbol of the British officer class and their understated courage. There is no love interest, aside from that between Gibson and his dog, who is run over on the eve of the raid. In its own way, *The Dam Busters* indulges in the same kind of British eccentricity that the Ealing comedies do, with its portrait of an underfunded military machine and an eccentric inventor who cycles to the airfield and has bicycle clips. Yet for all its occasional corniness, it is hard to resist when that Dam Busters march revs up and the chaps fly off into the wild blue yonder to do their bit for king and country.

The Cruel Sea (1953)

Crew: directed by Charles Frend; produced by Leslie Norman; screenplay by Eric Ambler based on the novel by Nicholas Montserrat; cinematography by Gordon Dines; edited by Peter Tanner; music by Alan Rawsthorne. B&W. 120 mins.

Cast: Jack Hawkins (Captain Ericson); Donald Sinden (Lockhart); John Stratton (Ferraby); Denholm Elliott (Morell); Stanley Baker (Bennett); John Warner (Baker); Bruce Seton (Tallow); Liam Redmond (Watts); Virginia McKenna (Julie Hallam); Moira Lister (Elaine Morrell).

This is one of the toughest and best of British war movies. It tells the story of corvettes in the Atlantic during World War II and rather than depict the usual unquestioning heroics represented in most British war movies, it shows the officers and men of the navy as anguished and afraid, at times weak. It also reflects some of the dislocation of the wartime years and its effect on marriages and family life.

Jack Hawkins in his finest screen performance plays the tortured captain with total conviction. This is not the usual screen Hawkins, all middle-class affability and high-mindedness, but a man uncertain of his duty and effectiveness as a leader and unsure if he can take any more when he is faced with agonising choices, whether to save his ship or sail over British sailors struggling to survive in the sea. It is this grittiness and realism that gives *The Cruel Sea* an unusual authenticity. War is portrayed as a grim business with little or no glamorous side to it. It is costly in human lives and the damage it does to those who survive.

Eric Ambler ensured that his adaptation of Montserrat's novel was superior to most of its kind and once again Gordon Dines' black-and-white cinematography leaves lasting images in the mind. This film was also the launching pad to stardom for two young British actors, Donald Sinden, who would later develop as a comedy actor, and Stanley Baker who plays an officer who has risen from the ranks and is faced with class antagonism from his public school colleagues.

Richard III (1955)

Crew: directed by Laurence Olivier; produced by Laurence Olivier and Anthony Bushell; screenplay by Alan Dent and Laurence Olivier adapted from the play by William Shakespeare with borrowings from Colley Cibber and David Garrick; cinematography by Otto Heller; edited by Helga Cranston; music by William Walton; production design by Roger Furse; art direction by Carmen Dillon. Colour. 158 mins.

Cast: Laurence Olivier (Richard III); Ralph Richardson (Buckingham); Claire Bloom (Lady Anne); John Gielgud (Clarence); Cedric Hardwicke (King Edward IV); Mary Kerridge (Queen Elizabeth); Pamela Brown (Jane Shore); Alec Clunes (Hastings); Stanley Baker (Henry Tudor); Michael Gough (Dighton).

This is the third of the Olivier-directed Shakespeare films and in some ways it is the best. At its core is an outstanding performance by Olivier himself. Undoubtedly over the top at times, his representation of the evil but charming Richard encapsulates much of the Olivier magic: his physicality, his wit, his scorn, his self-pity, a rare ability to speak dramatic verse with total understanding and realism.

The film was made on a restricted budget, which shows in the sometimes creaky sets and limited staging. However, the Battle of Bosworth Field, in which Richard is killed and Henry Tudor (Stanley Baker) emerges the victor and heir to the English crown, is impressively imagined, given the restrictions on extras. Olivier gives himself a wonder-fully hammy death scene, hard to resist for its sheer daring. During the filming of the battle scene, Olivier, always anxious to prove his manliness on screen by doing many of his own stunts, was injured quite badly when an arrow, meant to hit his protected horse, went into his leg: there-after, Olivier's/Richard's limp was for real.

Sterling support is provided by Claire Bloom as Lady Anne, whom Richard charms into marriage despite having killed both her father and husband. Cedric Hardwicke, for once, was given a decent film role as Edward IV, proving what a good actor he could be when he wasn't appearing in third-rate Hollywood movies. Ralph Richardson as Buckingham, Richard's close ally until they fall out, is terrific, as is John Gielgud as Clarence who ends up drowned in a wine barrel.

William Walton once again wrote the score, which has an Elgar-like gravity and pomposity. This underlines the reverential view of the English monarchy at the heart of the movie, despite the fact that almost all of the people involved in the struggle to seize the throne are portrayed as ruthless and cutthroat. Shot in Vistavision, the colour photography by Otto Heller is outstanding.

Incredibly, Olivier, nominated for the Best Actor award, lost out in the Oscars® to Yul Brynner in *The King and I*. Yul Brynner rather than Olivier? In *The King and I*? Never

have the Oscars® appeared more tawdry than in that
particular choice.

The Ladykillers (1955)

Crew: directed by Alexander Mackendrick; produced by
Seth Holt; screenplay by William Rose based on his own
story; cinematography by Otto Heller; edited by Jack
Harris; music by Tristram Cary; art direction by Jim
Morahan. Colour. 97 mins.

Cast: Alec Guinness (Professor Marcus); Cecil Parker (The
Major); Herbert Lom (Louis); Peter Sellers (Harry); Danny
Green (One-Round); Katie Johnson (Mrs Wilberforce);
Jack Warner (Police Superintendent); Frankie Howerd
(Barrow Boy).

This is one of the greatest of the Ealing comedies and once
again at the directing helm is Alexander Mackendrick, who
makes sure that there is an element of darkness to offset the
cosiness of this tale of comic crooks masterminding a heist
of banknotes. They use the rackety house of genteel and
dotty old lady, Mrs Wilberforce, as their hideaway when the
job has been completed. Posing as a musical quintet, they
persuade her to rent them a room for practising. The gang
consists of the crazy Professor (Guinness in elaborate make-
up as usual), a shady ex-Major (Cecil Parker as effective as
he always was), the sinister and choleric Louis (Herbert
Lom, never better), a teddy boy (Peter Sellers making his
mark in an early role) and the punch-drunk One-Round
(Danny Green).

   The real find of the movie is Katie Johnson as Mrs
Wilberforce, who was 77 when she made the film. Her role

could easily become too sentimental but the capable Mackendrick and Johnson successfully avoided this emotion. Eventually the gang manages to bump each other off and the police, in the person of Dixon of Dock Green Jack Warner, refuse to believe what they consider to be the fantasies of an elderly mind when the old lady tells them she has the money.

William Rose once again wrote a screenplay and celebrates British eccentricity and old-world charm. *The Ladykillers* represents a vision of a vanished London of tumbledown houses, loveable cockney characters, genteel old ladies who meet for tea and friendly police stations manned by sympathetic bobbies. Ealing Studios itself ceased production very soon after the release of this film, and soon Ealing whimsy itself would be a thing of the past.

The Bridge on the River Kwai (1957)

Crew: directed by David Lean; produced by Sam Spiegel; screenplay by Michael Wilson, Carl Foreman and Pierre Boule, based on Pierre Boule's novel; cinematography by Jack Hilyard; edited by Peter Taylor; music by Malcolm Arnold. Technicolor. 161 mins.

Cast: William Holden (Shears); Alec Guinness (Colonel Nicholson); Jack Hawkins (Major Warden); Sessue Hayakawa (Colonel Saito); James Donald (Major Clipton); Geoffrey Horne (Lieutenant Joyce); Andre Morell (Colonel Green); Peter Williams (Captain Reeves).

This is the first of David Lean's epic pictures, and can be viewed as an overblown pretentious piece of pseudo-moralising indulgence or as a serious and well-crafted film about the complexities and ambiguities of war. However, it deserves its place here if only for the scale of its ambition and the professionalism of its execution.

Guinness plays Colonel Nicholson, who is in charge of the British prisoners in a Burmese camp run by their Japanese captors. The Japanese commander forces the prisoners to construct a bridge over the River Kwai to aid the Japanese military. Guinness digs his heels in about petty matters such as forcing officers to work with the other ranks and endures torture and humiliation. He then has a change of heart and thinks it would be good for the discipline and morale of the soldiers if they built the bridge as well as possible, to show the superiority of the British in times of adversity. A raiding party led by a Major played by Jack Hawkins, accompanied by a surly and cynical American (William Holden), are landed nearby with the express purpose of destroying the bridge. When Guinness stumbles on their plans, he is horrified because the bridge, despite the fact that it will help the Japanese war effort, has become his raison d'etre. He is killed trying to defuse the explosives that will blow up the bridge. The Holden character is also killed, but the bridge is destroyed. The film ends with one of the British officers intoning 'Madness! Madness!'

The Bridge on the River Kwai tries to have it both ways: it decries the craziness of war but at the same time celebrates the courage and ingenuity of men at war. This ambivalence is represented in the Guinness/Nicholson character, but the issues become muddled and the film veers between two ideals. In the end, the Hollywood hero, although he dies in the attempt, brings about the successful conclusion to the mission.

The film won an Oscar® for Best Film and Guinness won Best Actor for one of his most mannered performances. Two of the screenwriters, who were uncredited on screen, Michael Wilson and Carl Foreman, were both blacklisted at the time because of the McCarthy hearings into UnAmerican Activities in Hollywood. Malcolm Arnold's score won the Oscar® for Best Original Score and Jack Hillyard deservedly won the Oscar® for Cinematography. It is ironic that Hollywood so garlanded the film when it was co-written by two blacklisted writers who had to leave America to earn a living anonymously in Britain.

Ice Cold in Alex (1958)

Crew: directed by J Lee Thompson; produced by W A Whittaker; screenplay by T J Morrison and Christopher Langdon; cinematography by Gilbert Taylor; music by Leighton Lucas. B&W. 132 mins.

Cast: John Mills (Captain Anson), Sylvia Sidney (Diana Murdoch), Anthony Quayle (Captain van der Poel), Harry Andrews (MSM Pugh), Diane Clare (Sister Norton), Richard Leech (Captain Crosbie), Liam Redmond (Brigadier), Peter Arne (British Officer at oasis).

By 1958, it was possible to present a more realistic and less heroic picture of World War Two than in many of the lightly disguised propagandist and self-congratulatory films of the war years and the immediate post-war era. The trend started with *The Cruel Sea* and *Ice Cold in Alex* continued it. Set in Libya in 1942 before the El Alemein turning-point in the fortunes of the Allies, it concerns the attempts of four British army personnel to reach safety in Alexandria in an ambulance travelling through a desert full of minefields, as well as German and Italian soldiers. The group consists of a near-alcoholic officer, whose nerves are shot to pieces due to prolonged exposure to danger, two nurses, one of whom is shot early on their trek to safety, a redoubtable sergeant-major and a mysterious Afrikaner whom they pick up on the way. They soon suspect, and confirm, that the latter is in fact a German spy. Nevertheless, they cooperate and survive many dangers before arriving in Alexandria where they have promised themselves the ice cold lager of the title of the movie. The British then protect the German by pretending they had picked him up as a stray prisoner and not as a spy, which would have meant his execution.

In covering up for the German spy, the British acknowledge their common humanity and their debt to him for their survival. West Germany was by 1958 an integral part of the Western alliance and on Britain's side in the Cold War, so the film was a reflection of changing attitudes to our former enemies. Nevertheless, it was an unusual plot mechanism for a British war movie to employ.

John Mills, the hero of many a war movie, portrays a soldier on the edge of total breakdown. Sylvia Sims is his love interest. Harry Andrews plays one of his utterly dependable, salt-of-the-earth non-commissioned officer roles and Anthony Quayle adopts an authentic-sounding Afrikaners accent to play the spy. J Lee Thompson admirably sustains the tension and the audience slogs it out with the characters as they face and surmount danger after danger. A Boys' Own yarn at heart, it is leavened with a substantial dose of realism and free of gung-ho attitudes. Above all, the characters are intent on survival and reaching the bar in Alexandria for that lager.

Room at the Top (1958)

Crew: directed by Jack Clayton; produced by John and James Woolf; screenplay by Neil Paterson based on the novel by John Braine; cinematography by Freddie Francis; edited by Ralph Kemplen; music by Mario Mascimbene; art direction by Ralph Brinto. B&W. 115 mins.

Cast: Laurence Harvey (Joe Lampton); Simone Signoret (Alice Aisgill); Heather Sears (Susan Brown); Donald Wolfit (Mr Brown); Ambrosine Philpotts (Mrs Brown); Donald Houston (Charles Soames); Raymond Huntley (Mr Hoylake); John Westbrook (Jack Wales); Allan Cuthbertson (Goerge Aisgill); Mary Peach (June Samson).

The British theatre had started to wake up with the production of John Osborne's *Look Back in Anger* in 1956 and gradually the British film industry latched onto the idea that working-class characters and life could be portrayed realistically on screen and still attract large audiences. *Room at the Top* anticipated the British New Wave by a couple of years in its gritty representation of sex, social climbing and the deadliness of life in a northern industrial city. The film brought a new frankness to its treatment of sexual matters and it was awarded an 'X' certificate by the British censors.

The story concerns a working-class young man, Joe Lampton, who sees no future in his boring job in local government and sets his sights on marrying the daughter of one of the local bigwigs, Brown. Along the way he has an affair with a married woman, who genuinely cares about him and whom he also cares for too. Despite his feelings for her, his ambition wins out and he abandons her to marry the rich man's daughter. There obviously was room at the top for thrusting young working-class men.

For once in a British movie, the class system that bedevils British life is confronted, and the snobbery and social barriers that are erected to keep the lower class in their place are foregrounded. Joe Lampton has the wrong job, the wrong education, the wrong background and the wrong accent for the mother of the young woman he has set his sights on; it is only with extreme reluctance that she accepts him into the fold.

It is an interesting aspect of this film that the adultress wife who has an affair with the hero is played by French actress Simone Signoret. She is not French in the original novel by John Braine. Even with this new frankness on screen, old stereotypes about the sexy French are played out. That said, Signoret is highly effective, bringing a warmth and sensuality to the part of Alice. Unfortunately, Laurence Harvey plays the working-class Joe. The new breed of British working-class actors such as Albert Finney, Tom Courtenay and Richard Harris had not quite broken through yet, so Harvey, who had box-office appeal, was cast. Donald Wolfit, however, gives a truly ripe performance as the industrialist. This was Jack Clayton's first full-length feature and he made a real success out of the opportunity it gave him.

Other Notable British Films of this Period

Night and the City (1950)
Gone to Earth (1950)
The Blue Lamp (1950)
Morning Departure (1950)
The Happiest Days of Your Life (1950)

The Tales of Hoffmann (1951)
The Browning Version (1951)
Laughter in Paradise (1951)
The Sleeping Tiger (1954)
Hobson's Choice (1954)
The Deep Blue Sea (1955)
Dracula (1958)
Look Back in Anger (1959)
Tiger Bay (1959)

The 1960s: The British New Wave

The French New Wave (Nouvelle Vague) directors such as Jean-Luc Godard, François Truffaut, Claude Chabrol, and Louis Malle had led the way in breaking free from the confining traditions of the established French cinema. Both in the radical new techniques and the subject-matter they dealt with, they created a vibrant, fresh national cinema. Influenced by that trend, new British directors including Lindsay Anderson, Tony Richardson, Karel Reisz and John Schlesinger broke free from the rather hidebound restrictions of traditional British cinema and made films that tried to reflect a post-war Britain, largely populated by working-class people struggling to make a living in sometimes grim circumstances. This change was also heavily influenced by the British theatre and the new playwrights (dubbed the 'Angry Young Men' by the popular press) such as John Osborne, Harold Pinter, Arnold Wesker, Shelagh Delaney and John Arden.

Lindsay Anderson and Karel Reisz had been involved in the 'Free Cinema' movement, making several documentaries that dealt with the class structure in British society and portrayed the working lives of ordinary people. Generally, the British New Wave was leftist in attitude, critical of the establishment and class barriers, although most of these directors who were part of this new impetus were themselves middle-class and ex-public schoolboys. Another change that the British New Wave brought about was the emergence of actors from working-class roots, often from the North. Albert Finney, Tom Courtenay, Rachel Roberts, Rita Tushingham, Alan Bates, Tom Bell and Alfred Lynch were not typical RADA graduates and could more convincingly play the working-class characters. Others such as Sean Connery, Peter O'Toole and Richard Harris came from Celtic backgrounds and brought a variety of accents to the British film that had hitherto largely been indifferently reproduced by actors brought up and trained in the south-east of England.

Traditional British cinema did not completely disappear, of course, but the 1960s are dominated artistically by these emerging voices. Commercially, the James Bond movies became huge international successes and the 'Carry On' series continued to be produced with ever decreasing quality as the films descended into total vulgarity.

Tunes of Glory (1960)

Crew: directed by Ronald Neame; produced by Colin Leslie; screenplay by James Kennaway based on his own novel; cinematography by Arthur Ibbetson; edited by Anne C Coates; music by Malcolm Arnold. Colour. 106 mins.

Cast: Alec Guinness (Lt Colonel Jock Sinclair); John Mills (Lt. Colonel Basil Barrow); Dennis Price (Major Charlie Scott); Susannah York (Morag Sinclair); John Fraser (Col. Piper Fraser); Allan Cuthbertson (Captain Eric Simpson); Kay Walsh (Mary); John Mackenzie (Pony Major); Gordon Jackson (Captain Jimmy Cairns); Duncan Macrae (Pipe Major Maclean).

With the British New Wave about to change the film industry, this more traditional British film stars established actors Guinness and Mills, in the story of the ructions within a peacetime Scottish regiment based in a bleak Scottish garrison town. Guinness plays Colonel Sinclair who has risen to his elevated status from humble beginnings, and has to stomach the appointment of an Oxbridge and Sandhurst officer (John Mills) to command the unit he has served in for years and where he has been his own master. Under Guinness' temporary command, military rules have been relaxed, discipline has become lax, and there has been a great deal of drinking and wild Scottish country dancing. Mill's character is an uptight martinet who tries to impose his will clumsily and fails to win the respect of his officers, most of whom resent that he is not Sinclair and too posh and English by half. After various challenges to his authority and Sinclair's various attempts to undermine him, he shoots himself, bringing about Sinclair's own mental breakdown.

Forget John Mill's Oscar® for playing the dumb mute in *Ryan's Daughter*, this is his finest screen performance. Here he wraps himself in the part of the neurotic, vacillating Colonel, who is no match for the combined machinations of the rebellious Scottish officers. Guinness as the working-class Scottish risen-from-the-ranks boor is harder to believe: he never disappears into a role and his Scottish accent is clearly adopted. Dennis Price is suitably reptilian as an aloof fellow officer, whilst Kay Walsh and Susannah York ably supply the love interest. Another wonderfully wry cameo performance is provided by Scottish character actor Duncan Macrae.

James Kennaway was one of the most talented Scottish novelists of his generation before his premature death at the age of 40 in a car crash. Adapting the screenplay from his own novel, Kennaway provides the director and the actors with some strong dramatic scenes, particularly when the two competing colonels slog it out. Underlining the themes is the question of what to do with full-time soldiers in prolonged times of peace. Another sub-text of the movie is the threat that the ruling class (as symbolised by the Mills character) feels from the rebellious lower class (as symbolised by the Guinness character).

Saturday Night and Sunday Morning (1960)

Crew: directed by Karel Reisz; produced by Tony Richardson; screenplay by Alan Sillitoe based on his novel; cinematography by Freddie Francis; edited by Seth Holt; music by John Dankworth; art direction by Ted Marshal. B&W. 90 mins.

Cast: Albert Finney (Arthur Seaton); Shirley Ann Field (Doreen Gretton); Rachel Roberts (Brenda); Hylda Baker (Aunt Ida); Norman Rossington (Bert); Bryan Pringle (Jack); Robert Cawdron (Robboe); Edna Morris (Mrs Bull); Elsie Wagstaffe (Mrs Seaton); Frank Pettitt (Mr Seaton).

'All I want is a good time. The rest is propaganda' is the credo of Arthur Seaton, the anti-hero of the movie. Stuck in a deadly boring job as a lathe-worker in a northern factory, he gets through his working day doing no more than he needs to, thumbing his nose at the Hitler foremen who try to keep him in check. Arthur lives for his leisure time when he can get drunk and bed women. He knows he is near the bottom of the pile and that the social structure of Britain means the odds of his changing his life radically are stacked against him. Yet he is determined not to become the passive automatons that his parents are or the obedient time-servers that many of his co-workers resemble. He becomes involved with a co-worker's wife, who falls pregnant and has to have an abortion. He is also attracted to a falsely genteel young woman who has ambitions to be married. The film represents Arthur's life as a struggle to keep one step ahead of the game and retain some kind of individuality and spontaneity in an environment that encourages conformity both at home and at work.

The film gives a richly detailed picture of northern working-class life, its strengths and its limitations. There is no doubt where its sympathies lie: at the end of the movie, Arthur Seaton re-emphasises his determination 'not to let the bastards get you down'. Alan Sillitoe adapted his own novel for the screen and he and Reisz are clearly critical of class-bound Britain, but they offer no real hope that things will change: the anti-hero seemingly has no interest in politics. Reisz, who was Czech-born, brings an outsider's eye to the themes and locales, and the film has pace and humour, and a real sense of sadness at the waste of human potential.

Albert Finney is magnificently cast as Seaton: brash, self-confident about his own attractiveness and feisty, he symbolises the working-class rebel who also limits his rebelliousness to the level of flouting conventions and putting two fingers up to his bosses. Rachel Roberts is highly effective as his married lover, as are Hylda Baker, Bryan Pringle, Norman Rossington and Shirley Ann Field in lesser roles. *Saturday Night and Sunday Morning* is a successor to *Room at the Top*, but is a much better movie. It brought an authentic frankness about class, sex, abortion and working-class life in general that the British cinema had never seen.

The League of Gentlemen (1960)

Crew: directed by Basil Dearden; produced by Michael Relph; screenplay by Bryan Forbes based on the novel by John Boland; cinematography by Arthur Ibbetson; edited by John Guthridge; music by Philip Green; production design by Peter Proud. B&W. 116 mins.

Cast: Jack Hawkins (Hyde); Nigel Patrick (Peter Graham Rice); Roger Livesey (Mycroft); Richard Attenborough (Edward Lexy); Bryan Forbes (Martin Porthill); Kieron Moore (Stevens); Robert Coote (Bunny Warren); Terence Alexander (Rupert Rutland-Smith); Melissa Stribling (Melissa); Norman Bird (Frank Weaver).

As a contrast to *Saturday Night and Sunday Morning*, *The League of Gentlemen*, released in the same year, is an example of the more traditional British cinema at something near its best. Any social comment inherent in the film is definitely secondary to its entertainment value and the cast is a roll-call of established stalwarts of the 40s and 50s. The plot revolves round a group of ex-military men, disgraced in some way and resentful about how they have been treated by established British society. Hawkins plays an ex-officer forcibly retired by an ungrateful army who brings together a gang of 'no-hopers' to plan and execute a daring bank heist. The gang will use the skills learned in their military training to bring it off, which he sees as ironic and only fitting. They manage to successfully stage the heist, but are forced to give themselves up when an old pal of Hawkins unwittingly leads the police to their hideaway. Even in 1961, crime still couldn't seem to pay off.

Hawkins is very effective as the mastermind, lending the role that touch of bitterness that he was so good at in order to leaven his 'good guy' persona. Nigel Patrick swans about the screen giving a Cowardesque performance; Richard Attenborough is a chap from the lower classes who is not 'quite the ticket', and Roger Livesey, that veteran of Powell-Pressburger movies, is terrific as a con-man specialising in vicars. Bryan Forbes, who wrote the screenplay, plays his usual junior officer role, whilst Robert Coote inevitably plays Robert Coote, the old man who leads the police to the gang.

The League of Gentlemen flirts with a critical stance towards the British establishment, but lacks real bite. Each character is given his particular psychological standpoint and if anything, it is all rather too pat and schematic. It is certainly a much better film than the Rat Pack's *Ocean's 11*, which followed a few years later and was surely influenced by this less-celebrated predecessor.

The Innocents (1961)

Crew: directed by Jack Clayton; produced by Jack Clayton; screenplay by William Archibald, Truman Capote and John Mortimer, based on the novel 'The Turn of the Screw' by Henry James; cinematography by Freddie Francis; edited by James B Clark; music by Georges Auric; production design by Wilfred Shingleton. B&W. 99 mins.

Cast: Deborah Kerr (Miss Giddens); Michael Redgrave (The Uncle); Peter Wynegarde (Peter Quint); Megs Jenkins (Mrs Gorse); Martin Stephens (Miles); Pamela Franklin (Flora); Clytie Jessop (Miss Jessel); Isla Cameron (Anna).

This is a genuinely eerie and frightening movie that gains its effects through suggestion and nuance, and eschews the usual shock tactics of routine horror movies. The film gains from its ambivalence about whether the events that seem to be happening are 'real' or the result of the repressed imagination of the governess through whose eyes we see them. Adapted from Henry James' ghost story by several screenwriters, the main credit for creating the sense of evil and foreboding must be given to Jack Clayton, the talented director of *Room at the Top*.

Deborah Kerr plays a rather prim and almost certainly repressed governess who is employed by Michael Redgrave to look after his nephew and niece in a large country estate. The children seem angelic at first, but soon strange undercurrents surface and the governess begins to see apparitions which, from her description, turn out to be much like those of the former and late steward of the estate and his dead lover, who had had a sado-masochistic relationship. They also had some kind of evil influence on the children and through the governess's eyes, we gradually see them turn from the angels they appear at first into the possessed demons they may be.

There is no doubt that the filmmakers want to suggest that these manifestations are the product of the governess's overheated and repressed imagination, but it matters little how the film is read. Generally, the movie avoids the more obvious clichés of the horror genre, relying on point-of-view shots and understatement to chill the viewer. When we first see Quint, the 'dead' steward, for example, it is a highly effective, hair-raising scene although all he is doing is standing at some distance away.

Deborah Kerr was never better than in this role; she is highly effective in portraying a woman on the verge of breakdown projecting her own repressed desires onto the children and the dead lovers. Michael Redgrave does not have a large part but is just right as the uncle figure who doesn't want to be bothered by any quasi-parental duties. The film was shot in the Sheffield Park estate in Sussex and the director and lighting cameraman make highly effective use of the location. At a time when Hammer Films were churning out their revivals of the Dracula and Frankenstein myths, laying on the gore and cheap tricks of the horror genre, *The Innocents* reminded us that chilling effects in the cinema can be achieved by less 'shocking' methods: evil that is suggested is always more effective than blatant special effects.

A Taste of Honey (1961)

Crew: directed by Tony Richardson; produced by Tony Richardson; screenplay by Shelagh Delaney and Tony Richardson based on the play by Shelagh Delaney; cinematography by Walter Lassally; edited by Anthony Gibbs; music by John Addison; art direction by Ralph Brinton. B&W. 100 mins.

Cast: Dora Bryan (Helen); Rita Tushingham (Jo); Robert Stephens (Peter); Murray Melvin (Geoffrey); Paul Dunquah (Jimmy); David Boliver (Bert); Moira Kaye (Doris).

As in *Saturday Night and Sunday Morning*, the working-class characters of *A Taste of Honey* seem defeated by their lot and live lives close to desperation with only alcohol and sordid sex to alleviate their limited existences. There is no sense that these people could change their lives by taking political action or breaking away from their limiting roots. This is a view of the British working class as envisaged by Shelagh Delaney who was only 19 when she wrote the play on which the film is based.

Director Tony Richardson tries to inject a kind of working-class lyricism in the underscoring, using children's street songs and also some rather fey dialogue between the young lovers, the 17-year-old 'ugly duckling' played by Rita Tushingham and a sailor. This is not completely successful and creates jarring notes in an otherwise realistic and rather depressing picture of life lived on the edge.

However, the film deals with some challenging themes for a British movie of this era: the young woman, Jo, becomes pregnant as a result of a one-night stand with a mixed-race lover and one of the main characters is a homosexual, dealt with sympathetically if rather stereoptypically. When the girl has her baby, the homosexual moves in with her and takes on the role of the house husband, though their relationship remains platonic. When the girl's mother is abandoned by her vulgar new husband, she returns and frictions erupt between her, her daughter and the homosexual.

Dora Bryan is very effective as the feckless mother, Robert Stephens totally convincing as her slimy paramour and Murray Melvin touching in perhaps the somewhat clichéd part of Geoffrey. Rita Tushingham had practically no professional acting experience when she was given the role of Jo and she repaid the faith of the producers. Occasionally straying towards sentimentality, *A Taste of Honey* is still an important movie of the British New Wave.

Lawrence of Arabia (1962)

Crew: directed by David Lean; produced by Sam Spiegel and David Lean; screenplay by Robert Bolt and Michael

Wilson based on *The Seven Pillars of Wisdom* by T E Lawrence; cinematography by Freddie Young; edited by Anne V Coates; music by Maurice Jarre; production design by John Box. Colour. 220 mins.

Cast: Peter O'Toole (T E Lawrence); Alec Guinness (Prince Faisal); Omar Sharif (Sherif Ali Ibn El Kharish); Anthony Quinn (Auda Abu Tayi); Jack Hawkins (General Allenby); Jose Ferrer (Turkish Bey); Anthony Quayle (Colonel Harry Brighton); Claude Rains (Mr Dryden); Arthur Kennedy (Jackson Bentley); Donald Wolfit (General Murray).

Many people consider this to be David Lean's finest movie; others consider that it is one of his most overblown and overlong epics. Whatever the merits or demerits of the film are, the responsibility must be shared among several important collaborators because this is much more than 'a director's film'. Robert Bolt and Michael Wilson's screenplay attempts to create a mystique about Lawrence whilst trying to psychologically account for why he behaved so oddly. Freddie Francis's colour cinematography makes the desert look ravishing but everything else too glossy. O'Toole's performance in the title role is mannered, at times bordering on fey. Solid acting support comes from Jack Hawkins as the devious Allenby, Arthur Kennedy as a cynical American journalist who sets out to make Lawrence a mythical hero, Claude Rains as a conniving diplomat and Donald Wolfit as a bluff military man.

The movie accepts at face value the Lawrence myth, that a minor British officer with little or no military experience could join together warring Arab factions into a highly effective fighting force that helped to win the war in the

Arabian peninsula. Evidence has since piled up that Lawrence's role has been much exaggerated not only by his own 'testimony' but crucially by the real life American journalist Lowell Thomas (the Arthur Kennedy character in the movie), who sets out to create the Lawrence myth; a myth-making enterprise that had Lawrence's full co-operation. In the film, Lawrence is interrogated by the Turks, who do not realise his identity. In that sequence of the movie, it is implied that Lawrence, after a severe flogging, is raped by the Turkish commander, an experience that sickens him and at the same time awakens him to his real sexuality; but these issues are raised only to be finally avoided. The Arabs, despite Lawrence's passionate support, are cheated of independence at the peace talks at the close of the war.

Despite these reservations, and its historical inaccuracy, the film has a certain grandeur and power. Shot in giant 70mm, the camera dwells on the vistas of sand and presents a feast for the eye, underscored by Maurice Jarre's emphatic and rather overpowering music. It is the overall look of the film, the use of the moving camera and the tricksy camera effects, that remain in the memory after the film has ended. It is a pure cinematic experience, but hardly a convincing picture of a complex historical character.

Loneliness of the Long-Distance Runner (1962)

Crew: directed by Tony Richardson; produced by Tony Richardson; screenplay by Alan Sillitoe based on his own story; cinematography by Walter Lassally; edited by Anthony Gibbs; music by John Addison; production design by Ralph Brinton. B&W. 104 mins.

Cast: Tom Courtenay (Colin Smith); Michael Redgrave (The Governor); Avis Bunnage (Mrs Smith); Peter Madden (Mr Smith); James Bolam (Mike); Julia Foster (Gladys); Topsy Jane (Audrey); Alec McCowen (Brown).

Tom Courtenay, in his first starring role, plays another bolshie, Alan Sillitoe anti-hero whose essential powerlessness finds some satisfaction in thwarting the hopes of the governor of the Borstal where he has been sent for robbing a bakery. The governor (excellently played by Michael Redgrave) finds out that Smith/Courtenay is good at cross-country running and encourages him to compete in a race with a local public school, hoping that he will win and prove something about the governor's liberal regime at the Borstal. In a gesture of defiance, the lad throws the race when it is obvious he could easily have won it. Like the Arthur Seaton character in *Saturday Night and Sunday Morning*, he refuses to collaborate with the governing classes and stays loyal to his proletarian roots.

The story is told partly in flashback and we learn something about the influences and pressures that have shaped the Borstal boy's life. Working-class life is once more represented as grim and unrelenting; only small victories can be achieved such as the deliberate losing of the race to spite the governor. As in *Saturday Night and Sunday Morning*, there is a sense that the lives of working-class people like Colin are mapped out for them and there is very little they can do about it. It is perhaps not surprising that the movie found such favour with the establishment newspapers and critics because, although the overall tone of the movie is pessimistic, nothing changes because of the actions of the rebellious working-class lad and the established order is only irritated by him, not threatened.

As in *A Taste of Honey*, director Tony Richardson indulges in some lyrical sequences, especially when the lad is running on his own in the countryside. When he is allowed to do something he can do well and he is away from the grim environment he was brought up in, he feels a freedom and a lifting of the spirit. Walter Lassally's cinematography has much to do with the overall effectiveness of the film, not only in the cross-country running sections but in representing the grim, day-to-day existence of the Borstal and the working-class environment that shaped the young criminal's life. Courtenay is first-class as Smith and solid support is provided by Avis Bunnage, Peter Madden and James Bolam.

Billy Liar (1963)

Crew: directed by John Schlesinger; produced by Joseph Janni; screenplay by Keith Waterhouse and Willis Hall based on their own play; cinematography by Dennis Coop; edited by Roger Cherill; music by Richard Rodney Bennett. B&W. 98 mins.

Cast: Tom Courtenay (Billy Liar); Julie Christie (Liz); Wilfred Pickles (Geoffrey Fisher); Mona Washbourne (Alice Fisher); Ethel Griffies (Florence); Finlay Currie (Duxbury); Rodney Bewes (Arthur Crabtree); Helen Fraser (Barbara); George Innes (Stamp); Leonard Rossiter (Shadrack).

John Schlesinger had already directed *A Kind of Loving* by the time he made this movie, but it was this one that really launched him onto the international scene. *Billy Liar* can fairly be classed as belonging to the less radical aspect of the

British New Wave as there is no specific political attitude at play in the film. The main character's frustrations can be read as the frustrations of any aspiring would-be writer stuck in the provinces and living amidst a family who thinks he's a daft layabout. In its representation of London as the magic escape route for the provincial dreamer, the film is very 1960s. The era of the so-called 'Swinging Sixties' in the metropolis was just round the corner and this film anticipates it, although the main protagonist, who works in an undertakers but who wants to write comedy material for well-known comedians, fails in the final reel to make the break and leave his stifling, provincial roots behind him.

Waterhouse and Hall's play had been a huge success on stage with Albert Finney in the title role. He was followed by Tom Courtenay, who also landed the part in the film; he delivered a performance that marked him out as an actor with real screen presence. Julie Christie as a freethinking, free-living young woman of the early 60s, also made her mark and the sequence where she wanders round the streets of the northern city established her as an icon of the British cinema.

The most memorable sequences of the film are Billy's fantasies, which are enacted with full production values. Schlesinger had a tendency towards gloss and glibness, and *Billy Liar* is hardly free of those characteristics, but the comic material is strong enough to withstand the occasional discordant note and the scenes that overstay their welcome. It was an era when the north of England, and Liverpool, were flexing their artistic muscles and challenging London's stranglehold over literature, theatre and film. *Billy Liar* is an interesting example of that phenomenon.

The Servant (1963)

Crew: directed by Joseph Losey; produced by Joseph Losey and Norman Priggen; screenplay by Harold Pinter, based on the novel by Robin Maugham; cinematography by Douglas Slocombe; edited by Reginald Mills; music by John Dankworth; production design by Richard MacDonald. B&W. 115 mins.

Cast: Dirk Bogarde (Hugo Barrett); Sarah Miles (Vera); Wendy Craig (Susan); James Fox (Tony); Catherine Lacey (Lady Mounset); Richard Vernon (Lord Mounset); Ann Firbank (Society Woman); Patrick Magee (Bishop).

Joseph Losey, the director of *The Servant*, was an American filmmaker who had been blacklisted during the McCarthy period in the 1950s. He took the route of several other Hollywood talents and came to Britain to find work. His collaborations with playwright Harold Pinter proved successful and none more so than in this analysis of aspects of the British class structure.

James Fox plays a rich upper-class layabout who buys a Georgian house in Chelsea and hires Barrett (Bogarde) to be his manservant and general factotum. Gradually, Barrett uses his influence over his 'master' to take control of the house, using Vera (Sarah Miles), whom he introduces as his sister, to seduce his employer. The latter discovers that these two have a sexual relationship, but when he is told they are not siblings, he nevertheless sacks Barrett. Left to his own devices, the Fox character sinks into degradation, alienating his upper-class fiancé played by Wendy Craig. Barrett and Vera wangle their way back into his life and by the end of the movie, the servant has become the master, the upper-crust gent is now dependent on him for drugs, booze and general debauchery.

What exactly Pinter and Losey intended to say about class issues through this tale of descent into the lower depths is not quite clear. That the upper-classes in Britain were ripe for destruction? That the working-class are associated with sexual debauchery, criminality and manipulation? The social analysis is not really that profound, but what is of interest is the 'atmosphere' of the movie and the fascination of watching the characters' power games. The film is largely shot within the Chelsea house, which adds hugely to the sense of a corrupt world shut off from 'reality' in which the characters play sexual power games, act out class attitudes and generally behave very badly.

Bogarde is effective as the Cockney man-servant, James Fox is very well cast as a man who allows himself to be manipulated, and Sarah Miles brings her own brand of sexual sleaze to the part of Vera. Pinter's screenplay, as with all his work, sometimes overplays its hand and becomes too heavy-handed. Douglas Slocombe's cinematography adds a great deal to the overall tone of the movie and Losey's direction is excellent.

This Sporting Life (1963)

Crew: directed by Lindsay Anderson; produced by Karel Reisz; screenplay by David Storey based on his own novel; cinematography by Denis Coop; edited by Peter Taylor; music by Roberto Gerhard; art direction by Alan Whitty. B&W. 129 mins.

Cast: Richard Harris (Frank Machin); Rachel Roberts (Mrs Hammond); Alan Badel (Weaver); William Hartnell

(Johnson); Colin Blakely (Maurice Braithwaite); Vanda Godsell (Mrs Weaver); Arthur Lowe (Slomer); Anne Cunningham (Judith); Jack Watson (Len Miller).

In the 1950s, Lindsay Anderson was something of an enfant terrible of the British film scene as a critic, documentary filmmaker and all-round scourge of the establishment, until someone gave him his first feature film to direct. His avowed Marxism gradually withered and died, and he was later reduced to the inanities of *O Lucky Man* and *Britannia Hospital* and directing revivals of William Douglas Home plays in the West End theatre. However, *This Sporting Life* and *IF* are testaments to his talents even though his rather scattergun social criticism seems more the product of the peeved outsider than the product of any coherent political philosophy, despite his protestations to the contrary.

This is another 1960s British movie that represents the north of England as nasty, grim and mainly brutish. Its background is that of rugby league, the working-class version of rugby, which is almost exclusively played and watched in the north of England. The antihero of the film, working-class ex-miner Machin (Richard Harris) gradually becomes a star of the local rugby league team. To achieve this, he has to act as a mercenary brute, because his role on the field is to wield the fist and the boot. His success fails to impress his landlady, however, a grieving widow (Rachel Roberts), who is locked into her frozen emotional state and will not emerge even after repeated efforts by the insensitive Machin to break through the ice. They become lovers but she does not give herself to him emotionally and he is unable to spark her back into life. Meanwhile, his strength is more and more exploited by the ruthless owner of the club, Weaver, a fact that Machin is aware of and which he rebels against in small ways. It all ends tragically and Machin seems to be caught in a web of macho attitudes and working-class grimness.

Harris' performance as Machin seems, with the perspective of time, more and more an imitation of Marlon Brando in his early days: the same hesitations, vocal mannerisms and physicality. However, Rachel Roberts gives a stunning performance as the widow and Alan Badel is suitably smooth and repellent as the club owner.

The political attitudes inherent in *This Sporting Life* are more up-front than they are in *The Servant*, say. The working-class locations are photographed with telling, grim realism by Dennis Coop's camera; Anderson directs with sensitivity and understanding. *This Sporting Life* has few, if any, laughs, and is remorselessly grim, but it is a social document of its time and well worth viewing.

Darling (1965)

Crew: directed by John Schlesinger; produced by Joseph Janni; screenplay by Frederick Raphael based on a story by Raphael, Janni and Schlesinger; cinematography by Ken Higgins; edited by James B Clark; music by John Dankworth; costumes by Julie Harris. B&W. 127 mins.

Cast: Julie Christie (Diana Scott); Laurence Harvey (Miles Brand); Dirk Bogarde (Robert Gold); Roland Curram (Malcolm); Jose-Luis de Vilalionga (Caesare); Alex Scott (Sean Martin); Basil Henson (Alec Prosser-Jones); Pauline Yates (Estette Gold).

Ostensibly *Darling* is a critique of the materialistic, status-obsessed, celebrity culture of the 1960s, but it is so much in love with the shallow world it represents that it loses some credibility. Why, then, is it included in this selection? Well, it is a movie very much of its time, which has a superficial attractiveness about it based on the slick screenplay by Raphael and the even slicker direction by super-smooth, often camp John Schlesinger.

The story is about the rise to fame and fortune of a model and sometime actress, played by Julie Christie. She is portrayed as a person without any depth or moral standpoint. She allows herself to drift in and out of relationships, careers and marriages, using her beauty to move up in society until she catches an Italian aristocrat. Unfortunately, the aristocratic life she is expected to adapt herself to proves pointless and she is represented as adrift in an amoral world and shortly to drown in a sea of boredom and apathy.

The two lead male characters are played by Dirk Bogarde and Laurence Harvey. The former stands for integrity and some notion of culture, the latter represents decadence and cynicism. Bogarde struggles to symbolise anything other than a rather boring journalist who fronts 'serious' television programmes about literature. Harvey is typically repellent, and his character is straight out of women's fiction: the type of cad who would ruin a girl as soon as look at her. In its portrayal of the London society scene with its over-the-top parties and camp followers, the movie reflects that it is more than half in love with the world it seems to be condemning.

Perhaps this is why *Darling* still has lasting interest. Its motives are so confused, its execution so jumbled, that it inadvertently represents the confusion that was so much part of the 1960s. There is so much posturing going on here, with a superficial quest for 'real values' and an apolitical analysis of what is wrong with the Britain of its time, that the film itself encapsulates much of the silliness of the 60s, as well as some of that decade's benefits.

The Ipcress File (1965)

Crew: directed by Sidney J Furie; produced by Harry Salzman; screenplay by Bill Canaway and James Doran based on the novel by Len Deighton; cinematography by Otto Heller; edited by Peter Hunt; music by John Barry; production design by Ken Adam; art direction by Peter Murton. Colour. 107 mins.

Cast: Michael Caine (Harry Palmer); Nigel Green (Dalby); Guy Doleman (Major Ross); Sue Lloyd (Jean); Gordon Jackson (Jock Carswell); Aubrey Richards (Radcliffe); Frank Gatliff (Bluejay); Thomas Baptiste (Barney); Oliver MacGreevy (Housemartin); Freda Bamford (Alice).

The Ipcress File was a big hit when it was first released in 1965. Its antihero is Harry Palmer, a truculent cockney who has been commandeered into the British security services after being found indulging in a spot of larceny in the army. In this, the movie reflects the changing class structure of Britain in the 1960s, with the old certainties about authority and subservience becoming more and more challenged. Palmer is constantly at odds with his 'superiors', who see him as a nasty, bolshie piece of work but who also need his skills to carry out their less than noble machinations in the swamps of Cold War intrigue.

The plot revolves around the disappearance of a scientist and a top secret file. There are many double-crosses and unlikely plot twists, as is par for the espionage genre. Palmer is out there on his own under the supposed control of his controllers who care nothing about his welfare. In this world, there are no good guys and the bad guys are only marginally worse than your own colleagues. This moral confusion stems from the original novel by Len Deighton and it lends the movie more depth than the average spy thriller. *The Ipcress File* is an antidote to the James Bond series, with its super technology and glossy production values. Harry Palmer is given much more humanity and ordinariness than Bond so that an audience can identify with his insolence towards his upper-class controllers and his solitary and unglossy life style.

The movie was a triumph for Michael Caine, whose limited acting talents are best suited to the range of emotions his character has to communicate. Faced with an indifferent script, director Sidney Furie and Caine decided to concentrate on building a picture of the antihero, Harry Palmer, in all his coolness and obstreperousness, and they achieved a resonance for the character that matched the spirit of the decade. What gives the movie some lasting merit, however, is Sidney Furie's flashy direction and John Barry's evocative score. Furie indulges in an orgy of unusual camera angles, distorted shots, gigantic close-ups and clever editing to add an additional layer of meaning through the very style. The unreality of the cinematic style reflects the distorted reality of the spy world.

Accident (1967)

Crew: directed by Joseph Losey; produced by Joseph Losey and Norman Priggen; screenplay by Harold Pinter based on the novel by Nicholas Mosley; cinematography by Gerry Fisher; edited by Reginald Beck; music by Johnny

Dankworth; art direction by Cameron Dillon; costumes by
Beatrice Dawson. Colour. 105 mins.

Cast: Dirk Bogarde (Stephen); Stanley Baker (Charley);
Jacqueline Sassard (Anna); Delphine Seyrig (Francesca);
Alexander Knox (Provost); Michael York (William); Vivien
Merchant (Rosalind); Harold Pinter (Bell); Ann Firbank
(Laura).

This marks the second major collaboration between writer
Harold Pinter and director Joseph Losey. Like *The Servant* it
deals obliquely with class and power games and the
destruction that sex can unleash. The story is told in retro-
spect by the Bogarde character, an introspective Oxford
don who is seemingly happily married but who falls for
one of his students with disastrous effects. There is also a
'gilded youth' figure, a young aristocrat played by Michael
York, who sparks off envy and competition among the
middle-class academics who befriend him. The accident of
the title is a car accident that the film starts with and comes
back to at the end, in which the York character dies.

Pinter specialises in sub-text, the real meaning that lurks
under the words his characters exchange, and sometimes
this 'Pinterish' style teeters over into pretentious nonsense.
The familiar element of using games and sport as a
metaphor for power struggles among men is also
frequently overdone, as it is here with a cricket match and
a free-for-all rumble at the home of the aristocrat. Yet
Losey manages to create a picture of academic Oxford life
and marriage that is convincing. It seems all is seething
under the surface, which in itself is something of a cliché,
but there is sufficient veracity to the representation to
make it intriguing.

Dirk Bogarde is suitably reserved as the repressed academic, Stanley Baker convincingly repellent as his colleague and rival for the affections of the young student, who is played by French actress Jacqueline Sassard. Once more in a British film, a French actress stands for sexual allure and worldliness. Vivien Merchant, who at this time was married to Pinter, and would subsequently commit suicide, is very effective as Bogarde's watchful wife. Michael York is Michael York, and Harold Pinter gives himself an acerbic cameo role.

IF (1968)

Crew: directed by Lindsay Anderson; produced by Lindsay Anderson and Michael Medwin; screenplay by David Sherwin based on a script by David Sherwin and John Howlett; cinematography by Miroslav Ondricek; edited by David Gladwell; music by Marc Wilkinson; production design by Jocelyn Herbert. Colour/B&W. 110 mins.

Cast: Malcolm McDowell (Mick Travers); David Wood (Johnny); Richard Warwick (Wallace); Christine Noonan (The Girl); Rupert Webster (Bobby Philips); Robert Swann (Rowntree); Hugh Thomas (Denson); Peter Jeffrey (Headmaster); Mona Washbourne (Matron); Arthur Lowe (Mr Kemp).

IF caught the mood of the 1960s like no other British movie of its era. It is a picture of a British public school which serves as a metaphor for British society; although given that only the wealthy middle and upper classes can afford to send their children to these establishments, it is necessarily a partial one. However, in its critique of authoritarianism and abuse of power, it says something about how the British ruling class clings onto its authority and nurtures, through the public school system, future generations who will take over the reins of that power in their turn.

Malcolm McDowell plays the rebellious Travers, sickened by the conformist attitudes that he is forced to adopt in order to survive in the ghastly community of the school boarding house. The House Prefects, to whom the headmaster and the masters delegate the task of enforcing rigid discipline and loyalty to the school ethos, are the natural enemies of Travers and his few supporters, and he is subjected to humiliating beatings at their hands. He has become involved with a waitress from the 'town', which is a major breaking of the rules. At the end of the film, Travers, the girl and his mates attack the staff and parents of pupils after the annual school prize-giving. When the supposedly liberal headmaster approaches the armed students asking them to trust him to sort out any problems, the girl coldly shoots him in the forehead.

The film embodies a kind of scattergun anti-establishment set of political stances, but do not look for any coherent political thought or strategy. A few months after it was made, the students of Paris rose up and challenged the authority of De Gaulle and the French State, but in comparison with the protagonists of *IF*, their politics were considered. Travers and company seem to stand for rebellion for the sake of it, sexual freedom and a general dislike of the adult world.

Shot largely in Lindsay Anderson's old school, Cheltenham, the film is best when it is representing the deadly routine of the enclosed school community with its communal baths, its dotty or worse schoolteachers and the rituals of school assemblies. It could be that Anderson was working through issues about his old school and attempting to imply a wider significance that the film cannot really sustain. He liked to represent himself as a man of the left, but he was never convincing in this role, as his later work sadly bore out.

The film owes an obvious debt to Jean Vigo's *Zero de Conduite*, and made McDowell a star, but top-class performances also come from Arthur Lowe, Peter Jeffrey, Graham Crowden and Mona Washbourne.

Kes (1969)

Crew: directed by Ken Loach; produced by Tony Garnett; screenplay by Ken Loach, Tony Garnett and Barry Hines, bases on Hines' novel *A Kestrel for a Knave*; cinematography by Chris Menges; edited by Roy Watts; music by John Cameron; art direction by William McCrow. Colour. 109 mins.

Cast: David Bradley (Billy Casper); Colin Welland (Mr Farthing); Lynne Perrie (Mrs Casper); Freddie Fletcher (Jud); Brian Glover (Mr Sugden); Bob Bowes (Mr Gryce); Trevor Kasketh (Mr Crossley); Eric Bolderson (Farmer); Geoffrey Banks (Mathematics teacher); Zoe Sutherland (Librarian).

Ken Loach and Tony Garnett had had their successes in television's Wednesday Play slot, with productions such as *Cathy Come Home*, before they made *Kes*. They brought their radical sensibilities and views to this subject-matter, turning a simple story of a boy who finds a kestrel and thereby some much-needed meaning to his life, into a representation of a working-class community in the north of England with all its restrictions, poverty (economic and spiritual) and harshness. This is not a sentimental view of the British working-class. The characters are not the salt of the earth or brimming over with the milk of human kindness. Billy Casper, the boy protagonist, is confronted at all turns with indifference and sometimes cruelty. Because of his lowly class background he is dismissed at school as unlikely to amount to very much; at home, he is subjected to harassment by his older brother who takes out his frustrations with life on him.

Billy's life is transformed, however, when he rescues a kestrel whom he looks after and makes a 'friend'. There is an inevitability about the destruction of the falcon by his brother because everything in Billy's life is programmed to failure and loss. The one sympathetic adult represented is a teacher who encourages Billy in his caring for the kestrel, but he is one adult among many who show Billy little understanding. There is an authenticity about the portrayal of working-class life that the vast majority of British movies lack. It is not all gloom, however, there are some humorous episodes, including the famous sequence where the bone-headed sports master plays out his fantasies about being a football star on the school playing fields. Billy Casper is the kind of kid who is always last to be picked when sides are being chosen at football and who remains unnoticed at the back of the class. In focusing on a boy like this, Loach and his colleagues are making an implicit statement about the waste of human potential that the British class system wreaks. Billy has potential as his care for the kestrel reveals finer feelings and a desire for higher things, but the odds are stacked heavily against him.

David Bradley who plays Billy went on to become a

professional actor and Colin Welland, who plays the sympathetic teacher, continued his film career to become the
screenwriter of *Chariots of Fire*. Ken Loach would continue
to become one of the leading lights of the radical British
cinema, more politicised and able than Mike Leigh, who
became the safe, comfortable so-called 'radical' director of
the establishment. In his later movies, Loach sometimes
strays into sentimentality when portraying working-class
life and his films can be more worthy than worthwhile, but
in *Kes* he avoided those pitfalls, crafting a key British film
of the 1960s.

Other Notable British Films of this Period

Peeping Tom (1960)
The Trials of Oscar Wilde (1960)
The Entertainer (1960)
Dr No (1962)
A Kind of Loving (1962)
Tom Jones (1963)
Girl with the Green Eyes (1964)
Zulu (1964)
A Hard Day's Night (1964)
The Knack (1965)
Help! (1965)
Alfie (1966)
Far from the Madding Crowd (1967)
Oliver! (1968)
The Italian Job (1969)
Women in Love (1969)

Surviving American Domination
(1970–1989)

The American Film Industry by the end of the 1960s had emerged from a slump and the 1970s brought new peaks of artistic and commercial success. Directors such as Martin Scorsese, Francis Coppola, George Lucas, Steven Spielberg, Peter Bogdanovich and Brian De Palma were not only able to make films that won critical praise but also brought huge box-office rewards. 'The Godfather' films, *Jaws*, *Close Encounters of the Third Kind*, *The Last Picture Show*, *Taxi Driver*, the *Star Wars* series and in the early 80s *E.T.* established these movie brat directors as the new kings of Hollywood and brought unprecedented profits to the studios.

In the face of this Hollywood domination, European domestic filmmakers struggled to hold onto a tiny percentage of box-office revenues. When Hollywood has 95% of the world film market, what chance has a British, French or other European film of reaching world markets and generating much-needed revenue for further investment? The French have tried their best to protect their film industry by insisting that a substantial proportion of films shown in French cinemas must be home-grown. The British have no such policy so at times the native industry has struggled to exist. American money is certainly invested in so-called British movies, but that intervention largely results in films that are made to appeal directly to the American market rather than dealing with British subjects mostly relevant to a domestic audience. Such films made during this period, that dealt directly with British material and did not pander directly to an American view of Britain, were largely funded by television companies, notably Channel Four.

However, some individual voices did manage to emerge and produce 'personal' films, rather than variations on generic material or movies geared to American audiences. Sometimes a film such as *Chariots of Fire* or *The French Lieutenant's Woman* managed to say something about British society and also find favour with audiences and critics across the pond. The hard fact was that British filmmakers, if they wanted to enter the big league, had to make movies that America liked. The British domestic market had long since ceased to produce sufficient revenues to sustain any kind of major film industry.

Performance (1970)

Crew: directed by Nicholas Roeg and Donald Cammell; produced by Sanford Liberson; screenplay by Donald Cammell; cinematography by Nicholas Roeg; edited by Antony Gibbs and Brian Smedley-Aston; art direction by John Clark. Colour. 105 mins.

Cast: James Fox (Chas Devlin); Mick Jagger (Turner); Anita Pallenberg (Pherber); Michele Breton (Lucy); Ann Sidney (Dana); John Bindon (Moody); Stanley Meadows (Rosebloom); Allan Cuthbertson (The Lawyer); Anthony Morton (Dennis); Johnny Shannon (Harry Flowers).

Whatever its many faults, *Performance* can at least be described as a film very much of its time. Set in the late 60s, it reflects much of that era's social dislocation, experimentation, foolishness, hubris and indulgence. Forfeiting narrative coherence (it is no worse for that), its meandering structure reflects the druggy, decadent world it represents.

The plot, such as it is, revolves around a petty gangster (James Fox) on the run from his violent colleagues. He hides out in the house of an ex-rock star who is going through a bad time and tries to make things better for himself by wholesale drug-taking and mechanical sex. Turner seduces the gangster, Devlin, into his world with the result that Devlin's 'personality' fragments, his sexual identity becomes confused and his world view is upturned.

Donald Cammell's screenplay explores issues of maleness, violence, what it is to be an artist, sexuality and what constitutes reality. Teetering on the edge of pretentiousness, it finally falls over. However, along the way, there are some arresting visual sequences, directed and photographed by Nichola Roeg who had been the cinematographer on Truffaut's *Fahrenheit 451* and Schlesinger's *Far from the Madding Crowd*. The first half of the film, set in a gangster milieu, never really merges with the second half, which focuses on the world of the rock star. Director and screenwriter seem to be trying to make some comparison between the gangster's violent nature and the rock star's inability to perform any longer, but the connection seems forced.

James Fox is convincing as the hoodlum who dons women's clothes under the influence of the decadent Turner. Fox was apparently so affected by his role in this movie that he had some kind of breakdown and only found his way out of the depths through becoming a born-again Christian. In the 1960s, Jagger was meant to symbolise everything that was anti-establishment or even diabolical. In reality he was a suburban kid who joined a group who discovered the effectiveness of over-amplification in the process of colonising black rhythm and blues and hitting the rock big time. In himself, Jagger was hardly dangerous, but his public persona is used in this film to suggest depths of decadence and drug-induced isolation and it works quite well. Jagger's acting abilities, however, have always been strictly limited.

Performance is as irritating in its pretentiousness as it is interesting in its experimentation. It deserves its place in this selection, however, if only for breaking with traditional British filmmaking and attempting to say something about the counter-culture.

Get Carter (1971)

Crew: directed by Mike Hodges; produced by Michael Klinger; screenplay by Mike Hodges, based on the novel *Jack's Return Home* by Ted Lewis; cinematography by Wolfgang Suschitzky; edited by John Trumper; music by Roy Budd; production design by Assheton Gorton. Colour. 111 mins.

Cast: Michael Caine (Jack Carter); Ian Hendry (Eric Paice); Britt Ekland (Anna Fletcher); John Osborne (Cyril Kinnear); Tony Beckley (Peter); George Sewell (Con McCarty); Geraldine Moffatt (Glenda); Dorothy White (Margaret); Rosemarie Dunham (Edna the landlady); Petra Markham (Doreen Carter).

This is probably the most famous and cultish of all British gangster movies. It certainly set the benchmark for violence in the genre and it perhaps has had an unfortunate legacy in numerous third-rate cockney or 'mockney' gangster imitations that the British cinema has spawned in the last ten years. The film sets out to be a determinedly unglamorous view of the criminal underworld, but in the process it somehow manages to achieve the opposite. It seems to make grittiness and viciousness attractive so that the apparent intentions of the movie are at odds with the representation.

Caine plays a London small-time gangster who comes to Newcastle to bury his brother, another petty criminal. In investigating his murder, he becomes involved with the local criminal boss portrayed by playwright John Osborne (*Look Back in Anger*). Warned to return to London, he ignores the advice and is soon the target of attempts on his life. Finally, he extracts a gruesome revenge on those who killed his brother.

It is a stew of violent sadistic behaviour where extreme macho attitudes at their most repellent are on display. However, the movie never makes its mind up about the main protagonist and his violent behaviour, so the overall tone is at best ambivalent, if not approving. If the initial intention was to critique male violence, that purpose somehow got lost along the way; there is a heartless quality to the film.

There is no denying, however, that it has a certain power and interest. Caine is suitably one-note as the avenging brother. John Osborne, the playwright who wrote 'Look Back in Anger', makes a rather camp crime boss and Ian Hendry is convincingly seedy as a really bad guy. The women are either adornments or figures of ridicule so from today's perspective the sexual politics are pretty dire. Caine fans consider *Get Carter* to be a key film in the actor's oeuvre.

Don't Look Now (1973)

Crew: directed by Nicholas Roeg; produced by Peter Katz; screenplay by Allan Scott and Chris Bryant based on a short story by Daphne du Maurier; cinematography by Anthony Richmond; edited by Graeme Clifford; music by Pino Donaggio; art direction by Giovanni Soccol. Colour. 110 mins.

Cast: Julie Christie (Laura Baxter); Donald Sutherland (John Baxter); Hilary Mason (Heather); Celia Matania (Wendy); Massino Serato (Bishop); Renato Scarpo (Inspector Longhi); Giorgio Trestini (Workman); Leopoldo Triesste (Hotel Manager); David Tree (Anthony Babbage); Ann Rye (Mandy Babbage).

Nicholas Roeg was certainly one of the most interesting British directors of this era and *Don't Look Now* confirmed what *Performance* had promised: here was a British director who dared to step outside generic material and deal with substantial themes. Whether his treatment of these themes is always more than superficially interesting is open to question, but Roeg's films always look good and are at least challenging.

The film has an arresting opening with the accidental drowning of the main protagonist's daughter and then moves to Venice, which Anthony Richmond's photography captures in all its mixture of mystery, opulence, beauty and seediness. Indeed, the city becomes a 'character' in itself as it affects the Sutherland character, who appears to have some psychic powers. The bereaved husband and wife meet up with two eccentric Englishwomen, who also seem to be in touch with another world, and there are sightings of a bizarre dwarf-like figure who appears to be wearing the same raincoat that the dead daughter wore when she was drowned. It all ends badly for Baxter (Sutherland) and the final scene of the film sees his funeral cortege sailing down the Venice canals.

So what is *Don't Look Now* all about? A superior horror film, in essence, it is almost certainly about much less that it pretends to be about. Sutherland seems to be stalking death and finally death catches up with him, but it is best to enjoy the film for its incidental pleasures rather than seek definitive meanings. It is determinedly anti-rationalist, superstitious and 'psychic' and is in that sense a 'new age' piece.

Both Christie and Sutherland give convincing performances; Sutherland is suitably restrained and free from the aura of smugness that at times makes him dislikeable. It is Roeg and Richmond's use of the Venetian location that stays in the mind, though, long after the details of the story have faded from the memory.

The Man Who Fell to Earth (1976)

Crew: directed by Nicholas Roeg; produced by Michael Deeley and Barry Spikings; screenplay by Paul Mayersberg based on the novel by Walter Tevis; cinematography by Anthony Richmond; edited by Graeme Clifford; special effects by Paul Ellenshaw. Colour. 140 mins.

Cast: David Bowie (Thomas Jerome Newton); Rip Torn (Nathan Bryce); Candy Clark (Mary Lou); Buck Henry (Oliver Farnsworth); Bernie Casey (Peters); Jackson D Kane (Professor Canutti); Rick Riccardo (Trevor); Tony Mascia (Arthur); Linda Hutteon (Elaine); Hilary Holland (Jill).

Roeg again teamed with cinematographer Anthony Richmond and editor Graeme Clifford to adapt Walter Tevis' science fiction yarn to the screen, and once more indulged his weakness for using non-acting rock stars in lead roles. Here it is David Bowie and those who like his act will warm to his performance; others may well demur.

Bowie plays an alien who comes to earth to find life-giving water for his parched planet. In order to pay for the building of a machine that will take him back to his planet, the alien helps found a corporation using inventions that he has brought from his planet. He quickly becomes head of one of the most powerful companies in the world. We then watch his gradual disintegration as he succumbs to earthly temptations, such as alcohol and television which he watches all day on numerous sets. An allegory, then, about capitalist society and materialism, and moral decay.

As with most of Roeg's other movies, the visual qualities are much more worthwhile than the rather overblown themes the movie aspires to deal with. There is much less to the movie than meets the eye, but what meets the eye is often intriguing and ravishing. Roeg is first and foremost a cinematographer, a design director, a kind of Vincente Minnelli of his period. His films are not strong on intellectual content, neither are they devoid of it. *Performance*, *Don't Look Now* and *The Man Who Fell to Earth* all have their intellectual aspirations, but there is so much 'dressing-up' and heavy underlining. Far better to enjoy the purely cinematic, visual elements. If style is meaning, then the real meaning of the movies he directs is in the cinematography.

At its original length of 140 minutes, the film is in real danger of outstaying its welcome, but at least the film-makers were attempting something out of the ordinary; even if they were only partially successful, the endeavour made it much more worthwhile than the vast majority of British movies produced in the 1970s.

Quadrophenia (1979)

Crew: directed by Franc Roddam; produced by Roy Baird and Bill Curbishley; screenplay by Dave Humphries, Martin Stellman, Franc Roddam and Pete Townsend; cinematography by Brian Tuffano; edited by Mike Taylor; music by The Who; production design by Simon Holland. Colour. 120 mins.

Cast: Phil Daniels (Jimmy Michael Cooper); Mark Wingett (Dave); Philip Davis (Chalky); Leslie Ash (Steph); Garry Cooper (Pete); Toyah Wilcox (Monkey); Sting (The Ace Face); Trevor Laird (Ferdy); Gary Shail (Spider); Kate Williams (Mrs Cooper).

This is British cinema taking on board 'youth culture' and attempting to represent the particular era of the 1960s from the viewpoint of working-class/lower middle-class lads aspiring to lead lives that would hold more excitement and variety than those of their parents. 'The Who' rock group voiced these aspirations in their music and acted as executive producers on the film. 'Mods' with their curiously conformist and neat style of dressing (the lads with their crombie overcoats and pork pie hats, the girls with their mini-skirts, long tresses and neat shoes) became associated with 'The Who' and it is this particular branch of youth subculture that *Quadrophenia* examines.

The film follows a group of Mods in their quest for some alleviation from the boredom of everyday life and humdrum jobs. They fetishise clothes and Vespas; style, tacky as it is, is everything. Posing and narcissism are all. The film is honest about the futility that underlines the existences of these young people. The characters that Phil Daniels, Philip Davis and others play are not stupid, but their life choices are restricted by their class background and education. The enemies of the Mods are the Rockers, determinedly working-class and macho in their style and dismissive of the Mods' effeteness. The two groups clash on Brighton beach on the south coast as they try to inject through these brawls some meaning into their otherwise pointless and dull lives.

There is a certain authenticity about the representation of the kinds of lives these young people live and the film does not, à la Cliff Richard films of the period, paint a jolly, rosy picture of the opportunities that existed for suburban lower class kids in Britain. For example, the morning after the running fights between the Mods and Rockers on the beaches of Brighton, the main protagonist spies one of the heroic leaders of the Mods (played by Sting) resuming his everyday existence as a bellboy at the Grand Hotel. He may be known as The Ace Face within his sub-culture peer group, but to his employers and the hotel clients he is merely a faceless youth who carries bags and who may be thrown a tip now and again.

Phil Daniels is particularly effective as Jimmy, and Franc Roddam directs with commendable pace and sympathy. How you react to the soundtrack by 'The Who' will depend on what you think of the group's music in general, but at the very least it is evocative of the period. *Quadrophenia* is one of the best movies about youth and youth culture that the British cinema has made yet.

The Long Good Friday (1980)

Crew: directed by John Mackenzie; produced by Barry Hanson; screenplay by Barrie Keefe; cinematography by Phil Meheux; edited by Mike Taylor; music by Francis Monkman; art direction by Vic Symonds. Colour. 105 mins.

Cast: Bob Hoskins (Harold); Helen Mirren (Victoria); Eddie Constantine (Charlie); Dave King (Parky); Bryan Marshall (Harris); George Coulouris (Gus); Derek Thompson (Jeff); Pierce Brosnan (1st Irishman); Billy Cornelius (Pete).

This is a tough, rather sadistic, British gangster movie that attempts to be about more than a bunch of psychopaths killing each other. The element that lifts it above the ordinary is the portrayal of the IRA and their involvement in the illegal machinations that form the basis of the plot.

Harold (Bob Hoskins) is a cocky underworld boss whose empire begins to crumble one Easter weekend. He is on the verge of concluding a crooked land deal with the American mafia when the IRA intervenes and start to dismantle him and his criminal organisation. To begin with, Harold thinks it is his rival London gangster bosses who are trying to destroy him and he takes ruthless steps to find out what is going on and to extract revenge, but gradually it dawns on him that he is up against a much more lethal grouping.

It is a corrupt Britain that is portrayed in this movie, where power belongs to the most ruthless and violent. The crime boss is as powerless to resist the violence of the IRA as are the authorities. The IRA are not glamorised and are shown to be willing to murder and destroy property to get their way. The film is high on a fashionable kind of cynicism but no alternative to these oppressive machinations are represented.

Bob Hoskins made his name with his performance in this film, enacting his rather repellent, aggressive cockney psychopath. The film, however, seems to implicitly encourage a sympathy for the character as his power evaporates, despite the fact that he is a torturing, bullying lunatic. The besetting sin of many gangster movies is to glamorise violent criminals and to turn them into anti-heroes. *The Long Good Friday* is hardly free from this criticism, yet there is a power and realism that reminds the viewer that violence and torture are not admirable.

Two cameo performances are worth noting: Eddie Constantine, the American actor who made many a French gangster film and worked with Jean-Luc Godard in *Alphaville*, plays the negotiator for the American crime grouping dealing with Harold, and Pierce Brosnan, future James Bond, makes an appearance as First Irishman.

The French Lieutenant's Woman (1981)

Crew: directed by Karel Reisz; produced by Leon Clore; screenplay by Harold Pinter from the novel by John Fowles; cinematography by Freddie Francis; edited by John Bloom; music by Carl Davis; production design by Assheton Gorton; art direction by Norman Dorme, Terry Pritchard and Allan Cameron; costumes by Tom Rand. Colour. 127 mins.

Cast: Meryl Streep (Sarah/Anna); Jeremy Irons (Charles/Mike); Hilton McRae (Sam); Emily Morgan (Mary);

Charlotte Mitchell (Mrs Tranter); Lynsey Baxter (Ernestina); Jean Faulds (Cook); Peter Vaughan (Mr Freeman); Colin Jeavons (Vicar); Liz Smith (Mrs Fairley).

The filmmakers took the decision to create a contemporary parallel story to underline Fowles' original tale of Victorian repression and ultimate liberation. Indeed, this modern plotline is a postmodernist self-reflecting technique, with its representation of the two actors playing the Victorian lovers in a film version of *The French Lieutenant's Woman*. The stars of the film are having an illicit affair just as the two protagonists in the Victoran sections of the film are, but the difference in the relationships between the man and woman in the contemporary tale and that between the 19th century lovers pinpoints the vastly changed status of women that a hundred years has brought. Anna, the liberated modern woman, calls the shots in the relationship with her married lover, Mike, and dumps him when the filming is over, whilst Sarah, the Victorian heroine is much more dependent on Charles, the liberal Victorian gent, although by the end of the movie, she has made substantial progress in carving out a more independent life for herself.

This parallelling of stories does not work completely, but it is a worthwhile attempt, and a testimony to the ambitions of Karel Reisz, the director, and Harold Pinter, the screenwriter. At times, the underlining of the parallels is rather heavy-handed, an aspect, despite its reputation for subtlety, of Pinter's writing. The Victorian sections are more worthwhile than the sequences in the 1980s, and the overall production design is excellent. Lyme Regis was dressed up for the filming to look like the authentic Victorian article; the scenes on the Cobb, the elongated stone jetty, are excellently photographed and the woods surrounding Lyme Regis are also effectively used.

At times theatening to become a period piece and a tasteful piece of heritage cinema, it is rescued by the authentic sense of sexual passion that is thwarted. Victorian puritanism and cruelties are strongly represented and the fate of women like Sarah, a disgraced governess who has been more or less ostracised by the Lyme Regis bourgeoisie because of her supposed affair with the French lieutenant of the title, is convincingly portrayed. Meryl Streep gives a strong performance as both Sarah and Anna, whilst Jeremy Irons has never been better on screen as Charles/ Mike.

Karel Reisz, a Czech ex-patriate, was one of the best of British directors and he makes sure that the bodice-ripping element of the story never overshadows its more intellectual aspects.

The Ploughman's Lunch (1984)

Crew: directed by Richard Eyre; produced by Simon Relph and Ann Scott; screenplay by Ian McEwan; cinematography by Clive Tickner; edited by David Martin; music by Dominic Muldowney; production design by Luciana Arrighi; art direction by Michael Pickwoad; costumes by Luciana Arrighi. Colour. 107 mins.

Cast: Jonathan Pryce (James Penfield); Tim Curry (Jeremy Hancock); Rosemary Harris (Ann Barrington); Frank Finlay (Matthew Fox); Charlie Dore (Susan Barrington); David De Keyser (Gold); Nat Jackley (Mr Penfield); Bill Paterson (Lecturer).

Made during the first part of the so-called Thatcher era when an extreme Conservative government was dismantling the trade unions, British industry and the public services, *The Ploughman's Lunch* is one of the few mainstream British films, with the exception of those directed by Ken Loach, to take on political issues directly and comment on contemporary events. In no way is it propagandist in tone or representative of one particular political stance. It is more subtle than that and gains its power through understatement and obliqueness of point of view.

Jonathan Pryce plays a journalist on the make with pretensions to being a historian. He senses that the Thatcher era makes the time ripe for a reassessment of the 1956 Suez invasion undertaken by a previous Conservative government. The film was made less than a couple of years after the Falklands war, so there are obvious, if unspoken, parallels made between the two invasions. Penfield, like most journalists of his ilk, shapes his political opinions to suit the times; he is a time-server, who wants to succeed in the world more than anything else and he is willing to dissemble, crawl and lie to get what he wants. He stands for nothing except his own advancement and in this central figure, the movie tries to say something important about the 1980s and the Thatcher era, when cynicism was at its most rife and the cult of the ambitious individual was most encouraged.

There is a telling moment at the end of the movie when the journalist attends the funeral of one of his parents. As he stands by the graveside, he glances at his watch. The funeral rites are an irritation, an irrelevance, to this emotionally and morally bankrupt man, who wants to be off somewhere else climbing the greasy pole. The filmmakers managed to shoot Pryce in the assembly hall where the Conservative Party were holding their annual conference, which adds an extra layer of authenticity to the movie.

Richard Eyre became one of the best directors to run London's National Theatre and it is a pity that none of the films he has made since *The Ploughman's Lunch* have packed the same punch or been as relevant to contemporary Britain. Jonathan Pryce is terrific as the repellent journo and Rosemary Harris does a nice turn as a historian with some integrity. *The Ploughman's Lunch* is one of the key British films of the 1980s and deserves to be much better known than it is.

The Killing Fields (1984)

Crew: directed by Roland Joffe; produced by David Puttnam; screenplay by Bruce Robinson, based on the magazine article 'The Death and Life of Dith Pran' by Sidney Schanberg; cinematography by Chris Menges; edited by Jim Clark; music by Mike Oldfield; production design by Roy Walker; art direction by Roger Murray Leach and Steve Spence. Colour. 141 mins.

Cast: Sam Waterston (Sydney Schanberg); Haing S Ngor (Dith Pran); John Malkovich (Al Rockoff); Julian Sands (Jon Swain); Craig T Nelson (Military Attache); Spalding Gray (US Consul); Bill Paterson (Dr McIntyre); Athol Fugard (Dr Sundesval); Graham Kennedy (Dougal); Katherine Krapum Chey (Ser Moeun).

The Killing Fields effectively and viscerally represents the horrors that the Khmer Rouge imposed on Cambodia in the 1970s, by creating the killing fields of the title and perpe-

trating the massacres of millions of Cambodians, a catalogue
of atrocities that has rarely been matched in the inglorious
history of mankind. The storyline revolves around the professional relationship and friendship of New York Times journalist Sydney Schanberg and his Cambodian translator Dith
Pran, whom Schanberg persuades to stay on with him in
Phnom Penh when the Khmer Rouge conquer the country,
even though it is highly dangerous for the Cambodian to be
associated with foreign journalists. However, Schanberg is so
intent on getting his scoops to send to his paper that he
neglects to think of his translator's welfare and the Khmer
Rouge take Dith away and send him to a brutal 're-educa-
tion camp' in the Cambodian countryside where he and all
the other inmates are subjected to a fascist regime of beatings, torture, interrogation and humiliations.

It is in this section of the movie and the subsequent
section when we follow Dith Pran's escape to safety that
the film gains its full power. The sheer incredible terror
imposed by the unspeakable Khmer Rouge, so full of their
own righteousness and veracity, is vividly and horrifyingly
conveyed. Whether an individual lives or dies is at the whim
of diabolically motivated children, whom the Rouge use to
weed out undesirables and the enemies of the proletariat.
As Dith Pran makes his way to safety, he encounters innu-
merable examples of the Khmer Rouge's utter ruthlessness
and murderous intent as they seek to cleanse Cambodia of
bourgeois impurities. Watching this journey does not make
for comfortable viewing for the viewer, nor should it.

A rather conventional happy ending is tacked on as the
two men meet again and then unfortunately the filmmakers choose to play John Lennon's 'Imagine' on the
soundtrack, a lapse into sentimentality that the rest of the
movie largely avoids. Nevertheless, the film works both as a

rather sombre entertainment and as a film that chillingly communicates what mass terror such as that imposed by the Khmer Rouge is really like. Much of the credit for this must be given to Bruce Robinson's screenplay and Roland Joffe's direction.

Dance with a Stranger (1985)

Crew: directed by Mike Newell; produced by Roger Randall-Cutler; screenplay by Shelagh Delaney; cinematography by Peter Hannan; edited by Mick Audsley; music by Richard Hartley; production by Andrew Mollo; art direction by Adrian Smith; costumes by Pip Newberry. Colour. 102 mins.

Cast: Miranda Richardson (Ruth Ellis); Rupert Everett (David Blakely); Ian Holm (Desmond Cussen); Matthew Carroll (Andy); Tom Chadbon (Anthony Findlater); Jane Bertish (Carole Findlater); David Troughton (Cliff Davis); Paul Monney (Clive Gunnell); Stratford Johns (Morrie Conley); Joanne Whalley-Kilmer (Christine).

Based on the case of Ruth Ellis, the last woman to be executed in Britain, *Dance with a Stranger* is a highly under-rated British movie that has much to say about British social attitudes, sexual politics and the judicial system. To its credit, it does not whitewash the Ruth Ellis character and turn her into a victim of male prejudice and class bias. Yet the film's sympathies clearly lie with the main protagonist because she is handicapped by her class background, limited education and propensity to fall for the wrong men.

One male in particular, David Blakely, is her nemesis; she gives him her love, but he finally rejects her because she is an

131

embarrassment to him among his socialite, motor-racing fraternity. Ellis shoots him dead and then waits stoically for the judgement of the court to be carried out, convinced that she thoroughly deserves her fate. The film makes no explicit case against capital punishment, but its opposition to it is implicit. Blakely is portrayed as a shallow, feckless, amoral opportunist, the kind of cad that mothers warn their daughters about. Ellis' passion is effectively represented, although never portrayed as a mere physical passion, more the need to possess and provoke an equivalent need in the love object.

The film convincingly creates the seedy demimonde of sleazy Soho clubs and the superficial kind of world that chancers like Blakely, with his pretensions to become a racing driver, inhabit. There is a sharp intelligence at work here with its eye for the snobberies and class barriers of Britain in the 1950s. Shelagh Delaney, the playwright who came to fame when she wrote the play *A Taste of Honey*, creates an almost hermetically sealed world with the skilled help of director Mike Newell.

Miranda Richardson gives a hugely effective performance as Ruth Ellis. Equally good is Rupert Everett as the callous Blakely and Ian Holm as the faithful inadequate whom Ellis uses to pay for her son's education and as a friend in need. Perhaps the grimness of the subject-matter has prevented *Dance with a Stranger* from achieving the popularity and esteem it deserves.

Defence of the Realm (1985)

Crew: directed by David Drury; produced by Robin Douet and Lynda Myles; screenplay by Martin Stellman; cinematography by Roger Deakins; edited by Michael Bradsell; music by Richard Hartley; production design by

Roger Murray-Leach; art direction by Diana Charnley. Colour. 96 mins.

Cast: Gabriel Byrne (Nick Mullen); Greta Scacchi (Nina Beckman); Denholm Elliott (Vernon Bayliss); Ian Bannen (Dennis Markham); Fulton Mackay (Victor Kingsbrook); Bill Paterson (Jack Macleod); David Calder (Harry Champion); Frederick Treves (Arnold Reece); Robbie Coltrane (Leo McAskey); Annabel Leventon (Trudy Markham).

Defence of the Realm is one of the best British conspiracy thrillers ever made and another British movie that deserves more esteem than it has hitherto been granted. It weaves plotlines involving a Profumo-type political scandal and a government cover-up about a near catastrophic nuclear mistake by our American allies to huge effect, creating an ambiance of secrecy, hidden forces at work in society, and paranoia. The movie gains much of its strength from the perception that the events portrayed are not that unlikely; indeed, recent governmental whitewashing and spin relating to the Iraq war only underlines how insightful the movie is.

Two Borstal youths escape and in their panic, one of them climbs the fence of a military airfield causing an incoming plane carrying nuclear weapons to crash land. Meanwhile, a prominent politician is caught up in a sex scandal with East German connections. The two seemingly disparate events are connected and journalist Vernon Bayliss (Denholm Elliott) stumbles on the truth. When he dies in mysterious circumstances, Nick Mullen (Gabriel Byrne), his colleague, is determined to uncover what Bayliss has been investigating. He comes up against the opposition of his bosses, the police and the security services. When Mullen finds out too much, he is eliminated.

The film communicates a bleak and cynical picture of Britain during the Thatcher years, when the Prime Minister was fond of referring to 'the enemy within' and the security services, as we know from subsequent revelations, were more or less out of control. There is no happy ending, the last shot of the film shows an explosion in Mullen's flat set up by the security services. There is scarcely a representative of the political, media and investigatory worlds who is portrayed as other than self-serving and obedient to the corrupt spirit of the time. The seekers of truth and justice are reporters, although both Mullen and Bayliss are portrayed as highly flawed.

Martin Stellman, who co-wrote the screenplay for *Quadrophenia*, wrote the screenplay. Director David Drury manages to create the appropriate paranoiac feel and the scenes in the newspaper offices are convincingly authentic. Gabriel Byrne is credible as the reporter; never playing for sympathy, he shows the limitations of a man who, almost despite himself, becomes obsessed with exposing chicanery. Denholm Elliott plays the drunken, has-been Fleet Street reporter as only he could, making this kind of burnt-out character his forte in later years before his premature death.

The Cook, The Thief, His Wife and Her Lover (1989)

Crew: Directed by Peter Greenaway; produced by Kees Kasander; screenplay by Peter Greenaway; cinematography by Sacha Vierney; edited by John Wilson; music by Michael Nyman; production design by Ben Van Os and Jan Roelfs; costumes by Jean-Paul Gaultier. Colour. 124 mins.

Cast: Richard Bohringer (The Cook); Michael Gambon (The Thief); Helen Mirren (The Wife); Alan Howard (The Lover); Tim Roth (Mitchel); Ciaran Hinds (Cory); Gary Olsen (Spangler); Ewan Stewart (Harris); Roger Ashton Griffiths (Turpin); Ron Cook (Mews).

This film deserves to be included in this section if only in recognition of its ambitions and visual qualities. Many people may find it boring and pretentious, but it cannot be ignored. It is perhaps Greenaway's most important film and it also represents that kind of non-narrative, freewheeling, art house cinema that has always been a strand of the British industry. Although the film certainly has its intellectual pretensions, it is basically an art school project with an almost total emphasis on decor, design, colour and the filling of the Cinemascope frame. What the film is thematically or philosophically about is much less important that its look. While the window dressing is beguiling, after the feast for the eye, it's debatable whether there is anything left over to sustain the mind.

The cook, perhaps, is meant to represent the artist. The thief symbolises the amoral, totally selfish and ruthless accumulator of power and money, a type lauded during the 1980s (Gordon Gecko from *Wall Street*'s credo 'greed is good' comes to mind). The lover stands for intellectualism, culture and a taste for the higher things of life. Sex and greed and money are all linked and the metaphor of food and appetites is heavily underlined. However, it is hard to pin down where the values of the film lie. Gambon plays the thief as a coarse self-made man, while Howard, impeccably academic and middle-class, seems to encapsulate moral values, and the two tussle for the favours of the thief's wife played by Helen Mirren. There is a class perspective to the proceedings with the lower classes portrayed as loathsome, a rather reactionary position to take.

The pleasure is in the incidentals, then, the non-thematic elements, what we might call the plastic qualities of the movie: the production design, the costumes, the high art backdrops, the dressing of the sets. It is an enclosed film which never moves away from the restaurant and the film tends towards the static, encompassing long speeches. *The Cook* is a highly flawed movie and one that divided opinion sharply.

Other Notable British Films of this Period

Ryan's Daughter (1970)
The Music Lovers (1970)
The Go-Between (1971)
The Devils (1971)
My Childhood (1972) *My Ain Folk* (1973)
My Way Home (1979): trilogy
Family Life (1972)
Tommy (1975)
Jubilee (1978)
The Tempest (1979)
Breaking Glass (1980)
Chariots of Fire (1981)
Angel (1982)
The Draughtsman's Contract (1982)
The Company of Wolves (1984)
Caravaggio (1986)
Distant Voices, Still Lives (1988)
High Hopes (1988)

Selling Britishness (1990–2005)

Periodically there appears in the British newspapers, articles prophesying doom and gloom for the indigenous film industry. The eternal question is aired: whether or not such an entity as a homegrown film industry exists at all, and if it does, what can be done to breathe new life into it. Then the corpse is revived with a big international hit such as *Four Weddings and a Funeral, The English Patient, Notting Hill, Bridget Jones's Diary* or *Billy Elliot*; the subject disappears from the newspaper columns, until the next time a features editor needs copy. In other words, the British film industry, it appears, is almost always in its death throes and unlikely to survive, and yet it always, somehow, does.

When in the 1990s Channel Four withdrew from large-scale investment in film production for theatrical release, further dire predictions were made about the future. However, with American investment on tap to bolster homegrown initiatives, most of the commercial hits Britain has produced have been largely financed by US money. Does that matter? Yes. In large, because the paymasters require product that will appeal to the American market and, thus, a pleasingly eccentric view of British society is served up, as evidenced in films such as *Four Weddings and a Funeral* and *Notting Hill*. They have little to do with contemporary Britain or the reality of life for most Britons. It is as though the British New Wave had never existed.

DON SHIACH

Aside from this 'charming' British eccentricity, also popular is a grim representation of the British lower classes as set in their ways, politically neutered and easy to patronise for their cultural *faux pas* and limited horizons. Hence the reason why Mike Leigh's films, such as *Vera Drake*, are a hit with Hollywood and Ken Loach's are not. If a Ken Loach movie is ever Oscar®-nominated, then something will have dramatically changed in Hollywood. Yet despite the pressure on British filmmakers to produce films that will appeal to the dominant American market, there have been a number of movies made over the last decade and a half that continue the British tradition of quality and which seriously represent British society without resorting to stereotype.

The Remains of the Day (1993)

Crew: directed by James Ivory; produced by Mike Nichols, John Calley and Ishmail Merchant; screenplay by Ruth Prawer Jabvala based on the novel by Kenzo Ishiiguro; cinematography by Tony Pierce-Roberts; edited by Andrew Marcus; production design by Luciani Arrighi; music by Richard Robbins. Colour. 134 mins.

Cast: Anthony Hopkins (Stevens); Emma Thompson (Miss Kenton); Peter Vaughan (The Elder Stevens); James Fox (Lord Darlington); Ben Chaplin (Charlie); Hugh Grant (Cardinal); Peter Eyre (Lord Halifax); Christopher Reeve (Lewis); Lena Headley (Lizzie).

This is probably the best of the Ivory/Merchant movies. Producer Merchant and director Ivory collaborated over numerous tasteful literary adaptations for the screen until

Merchant's death in 2005. Generally, these films such as *A Room With a View* and *Howard's End* are the cinematic equivalent of television adaptations of classic novels but with starrier casts and more money provided for production values. Mostly, they are 'tasteful' moderately entertaining and unchallenging fare aimed at a middlebrow and middle-class audience. *The Remains of the Day* aspires to, and attains, a level above most of their other movies.

This may largely be due to the source novel, Ishiguro's Booker prize-winning novel about native British fascism in the 1930s, class structures and emotional repression. The other factor that lifts the movie above the ordinary is the central performance of Anthony Hopkins, as the butler totally devoted to his calling who makes enormous and unnoticed sacrifices to keep the wheels of the big house turning. Brought up under the rigid British class structure of the time, and due to the nature of his job, he accepts without question that the aristocrat who employs him must know best about the affairs of the world, even when that involves his collaboration with Hitler's Nazi regime. He also denies himself any emotional life: for example, it his duty to go on serving dinner downstairs rather than being present as his father, the aged retainer, dies in an attic upstairs.

Emma Thompson plays the housekeeper who gets under the butler's skin and tries to unlock his feelings. When, years later, they meet, the butler has realised that his master was not the role model he thought he was, but it is now too late for any relationship between him and the former housekeeper, who has since married another man.

James Fox is suitably smooth and unpleasant as the Nazi collaborator aristocrat who tells the butler to get rid of two maids because they are Jewish. Peter Vaughan, who plays the butler's father, is outstanding. A scene where the son has to tell his father that he can no longer be allowed to serve at the table because he is too doddery is one of the most effective. However, it is Hopkins as the emotionally frozen butler that stays in the memory and gives the movie its charge.

Shallow Grave (1994)

Crew: directed by Danny Boyle; produced by Andrew Macdonald; screenplay by John Hodge; cinematography by Brian Tufano; edited by Masahro Hirakubo; music by Simon Boswell. Colour. 92 mins.

Cast: Kerry Fox (Juliet Miller); Christopher Eccleston (David Stephens); Ewan McGregor (Alex Law); Ken Stott (Detective-Inspector McCall); Keith Allen (Hugo); Colin McCredie (Cameron); Peter Mullan (Andy).

Set in Edinburgh, the film begins as a black comedy and then descends into a *grand guignol* thriller. Three flatmates, all professionals, interview applicants who aspire to become part of the flatshare. The three reveal themselves during the interviews to be superior, smug and rather cruel. They finally chose a dodgy character, who shortly thereafter expires from a drug overdose, leaving behind a case full of banknotes. After some deliberation, the three decide to keep the money. The rest of the film sees the dead man's associates track down the money and the three flatmates gradually double-cross and harm one another.

Shallow Grave is a very slick affair, perhaps too slick. It glosses over plot improbabilities to concentrate on the relationships between the three flatmates and the intricacies of their plotting. The action rarely moves outside the flat and a genuinely claustrophobic atmosphere is created; the viewer watches with an appalled fascination as these supposedly civilised, middle-class and educated individuals break every rule of friendship and integrity to get their own hands on the loot. Made in 1994, the film can be read as a comment on the greed and callousness that pervaded British society during the Thatcher and immediate post-Thatcherite years.

This is the first film in which producer Andrew Macdonald and director Danny Boyle made their mark and it also introduced Ewan McGregor as a rising star of the British cinema. Christopher Eccleston established his reputation and Kerry Fox also made an impression. *Shallow Grave* is no masterpiece, but its energy and ingenuity means it will remain one of the most interesting British movies of this decade.

Sense and Sensibility (1995)

Crew: directed by Ang Lee; produced by Lindsay Doran; screenplay by Emma Thompson based on the novel by Jane Austen; cinematography by Michael Coulter; edited by Tim Squyres; production design by Luciani Arrighi; music by Patrick Doyle. Colour. 136 mins.

Cast: Emma Thompson (Elinor Dashwood); Hugh Grant (Edward Ferrars); Kate Winslet (Marianne Dashwood); Alan Rickman (Colonel Brandon); Greg Wise (John Willoughby); Elizabeth Spriggs (Mrs Jennings); Robert Hardy (Sir John Middleton); Gemma Jones (Mrs Dashwood).

This film represents heritage cinema and the selling of Britishness to an American and international audience at its

141

most blatant. Here, however, it is executed with a certain amount of integrity and savoir-faire, and avoids the pitfalls that would render it merely a glorified television film. Emma Thompson won the Oscar® for Best Adaptation Screenplay as Hollywood gave the movie its nod of approval.

Thompson and Winslet play the relatively impoverished daughters whose marriage prospects are circumscribed by their lack of fortune and social position. Thompson (surprise, surprise) plays the sensible daughter whilst Winslet, equally unsurprisingly, plays the more headstrong and superficial young woman who sets her sights on the handsome Willoughby (Greg Wise). Each has to learn, in the traditional Jane Austen manner, that practicality has to be laced with feelings, and feelings have to be balanced by some rational thought not influenced by prejudice, gossip and malevolence.

Hugh Grant plays Thompson's love interest in typical Hugh Grant fashion, this time in Regency costume. Much better when he is waspish and satirical, Alan Rickman looks slightly out of place in the other romantic role. Ang Lee directs with discretion and Thompson's adaptation serves Austen's original novel well. Heritage cinema, but a worthy example.

Land and Freedom (1995)

Crew: directed by Ken Loach; produced by Rebecca O'Brien; screenplay by Jim O'Brien; cinematography by Barry Ackroyd; edited by Jonathan Morris; production design by Martin Johnson; music by George Fenton. Colour. 109 mins.

Cast: Ian Hart (David Carr); Rosana Pastor (Blanca); Iciar Bollain (Maite); Tom Gilroy (Lawrence); Pierrot (Bernard Goyon); Marc Martinez (Juan Vidal).

It is a safe bet that Ken Loach, unlike Mike Leigh, to whom he is often compared, will never be nominated for an Oscar® by the members of the Motion Picture Academy of Arts and Sciences. His movies are far too political for such a conservative organization, and deal with the working-class and the poor with a sympathy and lack of patronage that seldom finds widespread approval. Loach's first movies were made for the Wednesday Play slot on television in the 1960s and he had great success with *Cathy Come Home*, about a homeless couple, and *Poor Cow,* which focuses on the life of a working-class woman. However, apart from *Kes*, his films never reach a really mass audience. He struggles to find funding and is often accused of being propagandist and too left-wing.

That is not to say that Loach's films are faultless. Sometimes they seem 'worthy' rather than rewarding, programmatic rather than genuinely spontaneous. He has worked with many non-professional actors and actors who are not 'stars' because he wants to achieve that kind of authenticity that is rare to find from professionally trained actors. He is known to be very sympathetic to his actors and encourages improvisation, as does Mike Leigh, but the performances he elicits seldom turn into parodies or 'turns'.

Land and Freedom deals with that problematic theme for the British Left, the Spanish Civil War, and the role of international volunteers in fighting the fascist forces of General Franco. Those who rushed to defend the Republican cause started out with such high ideals and hopes that fraternal solidarity among the left volunteers would win the day. In the event, their side was divided, torn apart by sectional interests and narrow political objectives. It all ended badly and Spain was left to suffer under a fascist regime for the next forty years, partly because of these rifts. Many of those British volunteers who survived their time in Spain were left disillusioned and bitter. One such embittered veteran was George Orwell, who wrote about his experiences in *The Road to Catalonia*.

Loach's film does not dodge these issues, it confronts them head-on, which gives the movie an extra depth; it could easily have turned into a sentimental journey into the past intended to provoke regret about what could have been. Although the film does not totally avoid sentimentality, it has a hard enough edge to it, especially in the war scenes, that gives it a challenging tone. It is not a self-congratulatory poem for the Left.

Ken Loach has an even higher reputation in the rest of Europe than he does in his native country. He and his films deserve to be better known and reach a wider audience, but for those who control the production and exhibition of movies in Britain he is definitely a member of the 'awkward squad'.

Trainspotting (1995)

Crew: directed by Danny Boyle; produced by Andrew Macdonald; screenplay by John Hodge based on the novel by Irvine Welsh; cinematography by Brian Tufano; edited by Mashahiro Hirakubo; production design by Kave Quinn. Colour. 93 mins.

Cast: Ewan McGregor (Renton); Jonny Lee Miller (Sick Boy); Ewen Bremner (Spud); Robert Carlyle (Begbie);

Kevin McKidd (Tommy); Kelly Macdonald (Diane); Irvine
Welsh (Mother Superior); Shirley Henderson (Gail); Susan
Vidler (Allison).

Irvine Welsh's cult novel about the lower depths of
Edinburgh was adapted ferociously for the screen by the
Shallow Grave team of director Danny Boyle and producer
Andrew McDonald. At times, it seems intent, like the original novel, to *epater le bourgeoisie* with its insistent emphasis
on sickness, bodily functions, violence, seedy sex and
general Neanderthal male behaviour, but largely it has the
ring of truth of experience lived through, digested and
represented authentically. Whether its representation of
extreme macho behaviour on screen tends to glorify it or
make it amusing is open to question.

What is not amusing or comfortable to watch is Robert
Carlyle as Begbie, the most damaged of the main protagonists and a borderline psychopath, who most of the time is
on the edge of mayhem. Carlyle communicates the pent-
up, seething frustration and anger of the character bril-
liantly and this performance launched his successful career,
although too often since he has been cast as a 'head case'.
Ewan McGregor's career was also given another lift with
this film: his character is at the centre of the action and we
see the drug-induced hell of lower-depths Edinburgh
mainly through his eyes and consciousness. Never flinching
from showing the effects of hard drugs, the film simultane-
ously represents the highs as well, the reason why so many
young people without a sense of hope or future turn to
smack and heroin, and escape the horrible everyday reality
that surrounds them.

The film can reasonably be accused of having it both
ways: it shows the cost of hard drugs but also portrays them

as fun and life-enhancing. Each of the main characters are imbued with their own personalities and we are encouraged to see them as individuals, rather than victims or grotesques; the fact remains that most of the audiences who flocked to see this film, and enjoyed their antics, would give such characters a very wide berth in real life. In essence, the film is voyeuristic, allowing respectable audiences to wallow in the grunge excesses of Edinburgh druggies and no-hopers for a couple of hours before returning to their normal lives. Nevertheless, *Trainspotting* is a commendable break from the view of Britain served up in movies of the decade such as *Four Weddings and a Funeral* and *Notting Hill*.

Nil By Mouth (1997)

Crew: directed by Gary Oldman; produced by Luc Besson, Douglas Urbanski and Gary Oldman; screenplay by Gary Oldman; cinematography by Ron Fortunato; edited by Brad Fuller; production design by Hugo Luzyc-Wybowski; music by Eric Clapton. Colour. 124 mins.

Cast: Ray Winstone (Ray); Kathy Burke (Valerie); Charles Creed-Miles (Billy); Laila Morse (Janet); Edna Dore (Keith); Chrissie Cotterill (Paula); Jon Morrison (Angus); Jamie Forman (Mark).

Nil by Mouth communicates a raw intensity that could only come from the director and screenwriter, Gary Oldman, having lived through the brutal experiences the film depicts. Oldman, born in south-east London, clearly used his own youth as the starting-point for his screenplay, which as director he transmutes into a discomfiting, realist social document, unflinching in its take on the violence and abuse common in the working-class communities of South London. At the heart of the problem is a machismo that reacts to any perceived challenge to male status with pathological violence. Little tenderness is on display here, but then tenderness is above all what the macho male never wants to be accused of. However, Oldman shows that even the macho bully has his emotional needs and deserves our pity for inhabiting a prison partly of his own making, with the collusion of a society that discards any potential of such individuals and despises the sub-class it has itself created.

The causes of the violent behaviour of the main character (Ray Winstone) are never spelled out. There is no glib analysis of the factors that create a man like him, but the manner in which the environment is represented and the view of the limited parameters of experience open to these working-class characters signals that there is an implicit critique of society contained in the film. Their props are the pub, matiness, alcohol, drugs and a disdain for women. Personal responsibility for one's actions are perceived as important, but the social deprivation that these people experience in their drab and hostile environment contributes enormously to their predicament. That said, the film is never preachy.

Like *Trainspotting*, *Nil by Mouth* presents a picture of working-class life that gives the lie to the notion that in Britain we all live middle-class lives. The people represented in these films are the forgotten sub-class, only remembered when they cause 'social problems'. Gary Oldman made his mark in the theatre before he went into films and one of his first major roles was in Edward Bond's *Saved* at the Royal Court Theatre in London. He was outstanding in the part, bringing his own experience of South London to Bond's brutal picture of deprivation and cruelty set in the

same part of the city. In *Nil by Mouth* he once more delved
into his own life to produce this utterly unsentimental
picture of life as lived by many people in this situation. It
does not make for comfortable viewing. The domestic
violence is very hard to watch and the insistent atmosphere
of imminent mayhem makes for an unsettling film. Yet it
has its own integrity and you never feel that it indulges in
violence for the sake of it. Winstone is chillingly convincing
as the abuser and Kathy Burke equally so as the victim of
his domestic violence. Creed-Miles as the addict younger
brother of the wife is also outstanding. It is to be hoped that
Oldman finds another opportunity to direct again, using
material he knows about intimately. He invested some of
his own money in this film and it was money well spent.
The result is an outstanding achievement.

Ratcatcher (1999)

Crew: directed by Lynne Ramsay; produced by Gavin
Emerson; screenplay by Lynne Ramsay; cinematography by
Alwin Kuchler; edited by Lucia Zucchetti; production
design by Jane Morton; music by Rachel Portman. Colour.
144 mins.

Cast: William (James); Tommy Flanagan (Da); Mandy
Matthews (Ma); Leanne Mullen (Margaret Anne); John
Miller (Kenny); Jackie Quinn (Mrs Quinn); Michelle
Stewart (Ellen).

This is grim stuff indeed, offering as different a perspective
on contemporary Britain from *Four Weddings and a Funeral*
and *Notting Hill* as is possible, and it's none the worse for
that. Director Lynne Ramsay's directorial feature debut, it is

very impressive. She followed the film a couple of years later with *Morven Callar*, which, whilst not as successful in its own terms as *Ratcatcher*, still displayed an unusual talent.

Ratcatcher is set in Glasgow in a tenement block in the 1970s during a dustman's strike. Rats proliferate because of the rubbish; the vermin and the piles of refuse implicitly symbolise the quality of life of the people in the area. James is a 12-year-old boy in a totally dysfunctional family. His 'Da' drinks, is abusive and lives without hope, as does his 'Ma'. The boy inadvertently causes the death by drowning in a nearby canal of one of his few friends; unsure how to react to his actions, he is adrift in a harsh world where tenderness and morality are redundant. The film presents a relentlessly unglamorous and unsentimental picture of people living on the edge with no prospects of any improved quality in their lives because, the film implies, of the indifference and contempt the rest of society shows them. There is no sentimental 'salt of the earth' stance here; people living in this degree of poverty and social depriva-tion have no time or energy for anything other than bare survival. Eventually, the army is brought in to break the strike and clear the rubbish. People like James' Ma and Da are the products of this ghastly environment and society's callous indifference, but no political solution is offered in the film. Any personal salvation will be hard won by the efforts of hardy individuals like James.

Set in Glasgow, the characters' broad local dialect might be hard to understand for some viewers, but this should not put anyone off seeing the film. All the dialogue may not be wholly understandable, but the emotional thrust will resonate with those looking for more than superficial entertainment. There is humour amidst the squalour and the grimness, and the director and screenwriter never beg for the sympathy of the audience. *Ratcatcher* is the *Kes* of the 1990s and it deserves to be ranked alongside that key film of the British cinema. There is a truly memorable performance from William Eadie as the boy, one that recalls David Bradley's in *Kes*.

Other Notable British Films of this Period

Howard's End (1991)
The Crying Game (1992)
Orlando (1992)
In the Name of the Father (1993)
Four Weddings and a Funeral (1993)
Raining Stones (1993)
Funny Bones (1994)
Secrets and Lies (1995)
Emma (1996)
Brassed Off (1996)
Hamlet (1996)
The English Patient (1996)
The Full Monty (1997)
Regeneration (1997)
Welcome to Sarajevo (1997)
Little Voice (1998)
Velvet Goldmine (1998)
Onegin (1998)
Notting Hill (1999)
Bridget Jones's Diary (2001)
Morvern Callar (2002)
Dirty Pretty Things (2002)
28 Days (2003)
Young Adam (2004)
Spider (2004)

Vera Drake (2005)
Enduring Love (2005)
Yes (2005)

The Best of British

Top Ten British Movies

The Third Man
Odd Man Out
Black Narcissus
The Red Shoes
Richard III
The Fallen Idol
Lawrence of Arabia
The Lady Killers
Saturday Night and Sunday Morning
It Always Rains on Sundays

Top Twenty British Film Actors
(alphabetical order)

Cate Blanchett
Robert Carlyle
Tom Courtenay
Judi Dench
Ralph Fiennes
Albert Finney
Anthony Hopkins
Trevor Howard
Deborah Kerr

Roger Livesey
Vivien Leigh
James Mason
Laurence Olivier
Rachel Roberts
Peter Sellers
Michael Redgrave
Ralph Richardson
Margaret Rutherford
Alistair Sim
Maggie Smith

Top Ten British Directors
(alphabetical order)

Lindsay Anderson
Jack Clayton
Robert Hamer
Alfred Hitchcock
David Lean
Ken Loach
Alexander Mackendrick
Michael Powell
Carol Reed
Karel Reisz

References

Pym, John (ed), *Time Out Film Guide*, London: Time Out Group, 2004. (First published 1989)

Monaco, James, *The Virgin Film Guide*, London: Virgin Books, 1992.

Walker, John (ed) *Halliwell's Film Guide*, London: Harper Collins; 12th edition, 2003. (First published 1965)

Condon, Paul and Sangster, Jim: *The Complete Hitchcock*, London: Virgin Publishing, 2001. (First published 1999)

Sellar, Maurice, *Best of British: A Celebration of Rank Film Classics*, London: Sphere Books, 1987.

Index